DRESS LIKE A MILLION

# Dress Like a Million

# (on Considerably Less)

## A TREND-PROOF GUIDE TO REAL FASHION

### Leah Feldon

*Illustrations by Tamin Bressan*

*Villard Books*
*New York*
*1994*

All rights reserved under International and Pan-American Copyright Conventions.
Published in the United States by Villard Books, a division of Random House, Inc.,
New York, and simultaneously in Canada by Random House of Canada Limited, Toronto.

Villard Books is a registered trademark of Random House, Inc.

LIBRARY OF CONGRESS CATALOGING-IN-PUBLICATION DATA
Feldon, Leah
    Dress like a million (on considerably less) : a trend-proof guide to real fashion /
Leah Feldon.
        p.   cm.
    ISBN 0-679-41289-1
    1. Clothing and dress.   2. Shopping.   3. Fashion.   I. Title.
TT507.F433   1993
646'.34—dc20      92-31291

DESIGN BY BETH TONDREAU DESIGN
Manufactured in the United States of America on acid-free paper
9   8   7   6   5   4   3

*To my fabulous husband, Adam, for his love and unceasing encouragement,*
*and for the nineties woman. . . .*
*We have indeed come a long way.*

# Acknowledgments

My sincere thanks and appreciation to all those whose expertise, skills, support, and friendship have been invaluable throughout this project: My incomparable agent, Connie Clausen. All the folks at Villard, especially my doll of an editor, Emily Bestler; her assistant, Amelia Sheldon; Richard Aquan; and chief Diane Reverand. Illustrator Tamin Bressan for her wonderful drawings. Geri Cusenza, Erin Grey, Diane Smith, Margo Werts, Tracey Ross, Helen Murray, John Sahag, Deborah Raffin, Gayle Shulman, and Ronnie Carol Trugman for generously sharing their knowledge and experience. Lynn Roberts at Echo, and Rachel Bold at Calvin Klein for their kind assistance. Susan Joseph Goldman for her special encouragement. My pals, Cindy Pitou for graciously extending herself way beyond the call of duty; David O'Grady; Barbara Smith; Laura Torbet; Cheryl Slobad; Margot Dougherty; and my sisters, Eda Baruch and Debbie Kahan Kalos, for their brilliance and omnipresent goodwill. My brother, Jonathan S. Kahan for his caring and generosity in times of need; and as always, my mom, Henrietta Kahan, whose sense of personal style has never faultered—and who can still spot a bargain a block away.

# Contents

# Introduction

Ten years ago when I wrote my second book, *Dressing Rich,* the BMW was edging out the eagle as the American symbol. Yuppieism was at its peak. Banks were happily solvent, and junk bonds were king. The Reagans, both immaculately coiffed, were in the White House setting the mood for the nation. Spending as if you were rich, even if you weren't, was politically correct.

These days we're lucky to have a Pinto. Yuppies are washing dishes, junk bonds *are* junk, banks (not to mention Macy's and Bloomingdale's) are in serious trouble, and the national debt is beyond staggering. One choice L.A. joke touts a job as the latest Hollywood status symbol, which would be funny if it weren't so depressing. It doesn't take an economic genius to realize that most of us will have very little money to burn this decade—and those of us who do are not about to flaunt it.

But regardless of the state of the economy or any embarrassment we may suffer over our blatant eighties' consumerism, we still have to wear clothes —and we might as well look good doing it, as much for the needed morale boost as anything else. Looking good makes you feel better, as any psychiatrist would be the first to tell you—if you could afford one.

Fashion in the nineties is about individuality, practicality, versatility, simplicity, comfort, and of course, affordability. It's also about being easy. With all the other things we have to concern ourselves with this decade, fashion should be the least of our worries. It should boost our spirits, make our lives easier, consume a relatively small portion of our busy schedules, and even be fun from time to time. It should *not* be a major headache.

So my goal? To help you develop a look that is not only effortless, hassle-free, and relatively inexpensive to pull together, but also one that is in tune with the times; complements your individual personality, figure type, and life-style; and is packed with personal style.

*Dress Like a Million* has the word on:

- How to build the perfect nineties' wardrobe, with the right look for every occasion
- How to stretch your budget—and your wardrobe
- How to dress up *and* down with taste and style
- What and when to buy
- How to dress to flatter your individual body type
- How to discern fad from fashion, trendy from tacky, and classic from boring
- How to make great investment buys
- How to deal with colors, plaids, prints, and textures with imagination
- How to match your attitude with your style . . . and lots more

*Dress Like a Million* shows you how to use fashion, instead of letting it use you. It gets your creative juices flowing and replaces any worries you have about fashion with complete faith and confidence in your taste.

My favorite Liz Claiborne ad reads "Dressing Well Is Like Living Well. Sometimes You Have to Improvise." I think she hit the nail right on the head. This decade we're going to have to put ourselves together with more imagination and less cash, and that means fine-tuning our improvisational skills . . . which is just what *Dress Like a Million* is about. So let's get started.

DRESS LIKE A MILLION

# CHAPTER 1

# Current Looks du Jour

TRENDS, FADS, ATTITUDES, AND OTHER THREATS

The nineties may not go down in history as economic fat years, but there's still a lot to be grateful for, not the least of which is that no one, thank God, is telling us what to wear anymore. Right up until the last few decades you either dressed by the rules or got booted out of the corps. In the 1964 edition of *Elegance,* one of my all-time favorite fashion tomes, former Parisian couturier, Genevieve A. Dariaux, warned her readers that it was "absolutely unaesthetic and vulgar to wear slacks on a city street, even in a raging snowstorm!" (My exclamation mark.) She also noted that she didn't know "a single elegant woman"—skinny ones included—who didn't wear a girdle under her city clothes, and cautioned that the only thing that could destroy the charm of the ideal working outfit was "a provocative brassiere." *Elegance* offered a lot more unforgettable advice that I'd love to share with you, but I think you get the point: rules, rules, rules.

Needless to say, it was only a few cosmic seconds after Ms. Dariaux's book hit the stands that pantsuits became the rage, feminists burned their bras and chucked their girdles, and Woodstockians pranced around in nothing at all. It was the beginning of a whole new era.

## TRENDS—JUST SAY NO . . . SOMETIMES

Today, thankfully, there are no *obligatory* styles. There are still trends, of course, but you are not *obliged* to follow them. In fact, following them too

3

closely usually results in sartorial tragedy—as well as providing the fodder for *Glamour* don'ts.

Not that trends are all bad. In fact, you have to be aware of fashion's *general* directional trends or you'll find yourself totally out of sync with the times. You don't want to be tooling around in psychedelic granny dresses while the rest of the civilized world has moved on to straight-legged jeans and blazers. So it's important to keep in touch with fashion's prevailing moods and shapes. It's the *fads* you have to watch out for. They can be lethal to your image.

Fads are like bleeps in a trend. They're extremely short-lived and can be mildly annoying. While trends constitute the big picture—as in a *trend* toward simplicity or a *trend* toward a more structured look—fads are magnified snippets of a whole idea. Example: There is currently an ongoing mini-trend back to traditional femininity. We've proved, it seems, that we can wear minimal underwear and makeup and dress like little working men if we want to. Now that that's done, we can dress like "real women" again—if we feel like it. In fact we can even flaunt it. Resulting *fads:* lingerie as outerwear, false eyelashes, and ads featuring Marilyn Monroe look-alikes. They're exaggerated snippets of the *idea* of old-time femininity.

One of the keys to dressing like a million is seeing the big picture and staying current *without* sacrificing your individuality to fads or nominal trends. Which is not to say avoid them altogether. Some can provide a good laugh, others can add new life to old standards, and some might actually prove to have longtime fashion potential. So picking up on a trend or fad occasionally is fine—especially if it complements your particular style or expresses your heartfelt point of view. The warning here is not to subscribe to the latest rage simply because, like Mt. Everest, it's there, or worse yet, because everyone else is doing it and you don't want to feel left out. Unless a specific trend or fad suits you to a tee, or you can think of some ingenious personal way to wear it, forget about it. It would be a shame to fritter away big chunks of hard-earned money on some trendy number that will be out of style before you can get it to the cleaner's. Spend petty cash on fads if you will, but invest your serious money in classic quality items that will serve you well for years to come.

The bottom line is to see trends and fads for what they truly are, and not take them *too* seriously or interpret them *too* literally. Many simply exist as a reflection of the times and are not meant to be serious wardrobe contenders. The recent couture microtrend of la mode destroy, for example, which had a few of Europe's more avant-garde designers holding their shows in seedy, abandoned lots and showing clothes with exposed frayed linings, sleeves ripped off, raw edges, moth holes, and hacked-off bottoms, was probably, as *Vogue* suggested, more symbolic of "the ravaged landscape of the economy" than something you'd actually want to wear to lunch with your boss.

Other fads are conceived on a whim or by the media. When Madonna dons cutoffs and a bullet bra—or whatever her latest costume du jour is—she's dressing for effect, having a good chuckle, and is, well, just being Madonna. If you try to dress like Madonna you'll look like a pseudo-Madonna caricature, which, trust me, packs quite a different punch. (Also, let's not forget that Madonna has a delicious sixty-million-dollar contract and can do any old thing she wants.)

Individual style is about doing your own thing, not someone else's. It's taking bits and pieces of what's available and putting them together in your own personal way, breathing your own life into them.

## YOUR CLOTHES ARE TALKING . . . DO YOU KNOW WHAT THEY'RE SAYING?

Clothing has always been a language unto itself. In the days of yore, one's silks and satins proclaimed affluence, class, and education—to a manor wellborn. Rough unbleached cottons, on the other hand, said peasant. Today clothing is even chattier—now it has *attitude*. These days it's not just *what* you wear that conveys messages, but *how* you wear it as well. Take a simple white T-shirt, for instance. By itself it says "everyman." Roll up the sleeves and it says "active and fashion savvy." Iron it and it says "neat and fastidious."

What you put with what counts too. If you wear your high-top Reeboks with a strapless evening dress, à la Cybill Shepherd at one of her Academy Awards ceremony appearances, you're saying something quite different than when you wear them with workout clothes. It's more of a "screw you, I'll play your little game, but on my own terms" attitude, than one of health, fun, and sports.

And in subtle ways your clothes also send signals about your age. There are certainly no strict rules about proper attire for specific age groups these days, but we do seem to have a natural tendency to favor certain styles at different stages in our lives. In our youth we are traditionally more interested in the latest hottest items. Quantity is more important than quality, and the underlying theme is style over substance. During our twenties there's a gradual mellowing out; what's hot is interesting but not crucial to survival. When we reach our thirties our fashion tastes are more sophisti-

Bas couture is hip,
Hollywood, happening
. . . and risky unless you
have just the right attitude
to carry it off.

cated and creative. And when we're forty plus, comfort becomes a priority, quality a necessity, and our style and confidence peak.

Not that we *consciously* follow this route or are even aware of it, but it's there, which is why a black lace spandex catsuit might be amusing on a nineteen-year-old, but is almost always deadly on a fifty-five-year-old—even if she does have a great body. On an older woman the catsuit would indicate hip sex kitten aspirations, and probably fear of aging. Why try to be a kitten when you're a cat? Why compete with teenagers at fifty-five? What's the point? By the time we're into our fifties we've had time to develop plenty of other qualities that are a lot more impressive than breasts and buttocks— wisdom, insight, and intelligence, for instance. Better to let our clothes reflect our self-respect than mirror any insecurities.

I'm not suggesting that we have to raid our grandmothers' closets the minute we hit fifty. Hardly. There's plenty of clothing on the market today that is suitable for all ages. Anybody can wear jeans, slouchy jackets, T-shirts, short skirts, even leggings, if it suits her body. The bottom line is simply this: The older you are, the riskier pop trends and fads become.

Because fashion today has so much attitude potential and can say so much about us, we want to be doubly sure that our clothing is working for us— and sending the messages we *want* to relay. So let's start out here by analyzing some of the major directional trends of the nineties to see what they're saying, what they have to offer, and how much attention we actually want to pay to them. Some of them are more fad than fashion, while others proffer solid direction for the future. But they all carry lots of attitude and deliver very specific messages . . . and there's *something* to be learned from each of them—even if it's what *not* to do.

## THE FIVE CORNERS OF TODAY'S FASHION

### Bas Couture

Bas Couture, as the French would call it if they had thought of it, is *dressing down,* and since almost all of young Hollywood dresses this way at least some of the time, it's considered a very hip look. Bas (pronounced *bah*) couture literally means "down" or "low" fashion, and is, of course, the opposite of haute couture, which as everybody knows means high fashion. (Actually, even haute couture is getting rather *bas* these days.)

Bas couture is studied casualness: "distressed" jeans, thrift store frocks, Doc Martens, overlarge clothes, mismatched styles, unmatched textures, a blend of eras, and any combination or mixture thereof. Even retro, from the twenties through the seventies, is a variation of bas. There are different degrees of dressing down. It runs the gamut from light bas, which can be as simple as a loose, floral, rayon dress nipped in a bit in the back by two little clasps attached by an elastic band, worn with white Keds and socks, to extreme bas, which is epitomized by the young rappers Kris Kross, who wear all their hip-hop duds backwards.

In general though, bas is simply a semidisheveled, studiously nonchalant, occasionally uncombed, sometimes shabby way of dressing that is supposed to look hastily thrown together on a shoestring but can take a lot of hours and dollars to pull off. Think grunge.

Bas is everywhere. Sinéad O'Connor is perhaps the epitome of it, but even an avowed clotheshorse like Cher hangs up her Bob Mackies and gets *down* now and then. In a recent edition of *Architectural Digest* she is pictured lounging on the window seat in her fabulous new multimillion dollar Aspen digs dressed in faded, ripped-at-the-knee, frayed-hem jeans. Cher may be extremely rich, but she's a real person too, which, or course, is one of bas's underlying messages. Other messages are (1) I have a lot more to think about than how I look, and (2) I'm so gorgeous that I look fabulous in anything (and you don't).

The young Hollywood bas crowd could also be dressing down because they feel guilty for making amounts of money so disproportionate to their talents. But that's just a guess. Whatever, the truth is that most women who manage to pull this look off have great proportions (see next chapter), a good fashion sense, and would look lovely in last night's dirty tablecloth. How bad can Julia Roberts, Michelle Pfeiffer, Daryl Hannah, Geena Davis, or Winona Ryder look, for heaven's sake?

Like all trends, bas has some good points about it, and some that are not so good:

*Pros:*
1. While it's possible to spend a lot of money dressing down, you can do it very nicely on the cheap once you understand fashion fundamentals (which are coming right up in the next few chapters).
2. Since anything goes, bas can be *totally* comfortable.
3. It's a great look for travel to third world countries where looking poor is bonding and looking rich is asking for trouble.
4. Bas is relatively low maintenance. If something needs cleaning you can just throw it away, and rips and tears add just the right soupçon of character that turns ordinary old clothes into fab new distressed ones.
5. Since the choices are wide open there's definitely room for individual style.

*Cons:*

1. Proportions are tricky. It's one thing to throw old shapeless garments on a perfect body, quite another to drape them on one that is less than ideal. The better proportioned your body, the better this look works.
2. Bas is not a great boardroom look. Corporate thinking leaves no room for nuances. You could get handed a mop and bucket.
3. When it comes right down to it, bas works best when you're famous.

Credits and thank yous: Diane Keaton, the grandmother of bas; all those sixties hippies (for their free adventuresome spirit), *thirtysomething,* the brat pack and Sinéad O'Connor.

## MTV Chic

MTV chic is, of course, inspired by what could be called modern music, mainly hard rock and heavy metal. Where bas is sort of a modern movie star look, MTV chic is part and parcel of today's nutty rock scene where youth is revered and age is a novelty. In fact, even though variations on this theme often grace the pages of *Vogue,* it *is* a look best suited for women just past the age of puberty. Regardless of chronology, however, you can still rate the success of an outfit by how high it would drive your father's blood pressure if he saw you leave the house in it.

MTV chic ensembles (and I use the term "ensembles" loosely) are usually skintight. Spandex, Lycra, leather, and lace are the main fabrics de choix. Black is the *only* truly acceptable color. Lipstick is red or red or red. Stretch ultra microminis, bras and bustiers, metal-studded motorcycle jackets, and spike heels are wardrobe staples. You could think of this as Maidenform meets Hell's Angels.

As for messages, MTV chic says four things loud and clear: (1) I am very young or want to be. (2) I am a victim de la mode willing to look hip at any price. (3) I have a complete lack of individual style, and (4) I want to look tough, but I'm really insecure and not all that bright either. However, as always, there are some saving graces.

*Pros:*

1. MTV chic is a super dieting technique since every olive shows, and most clothes are either too uncomfortable or too revealing to sit and eat in. Also eating is counterproductive since it tends to smear heavy lipstick.
2. Black is not only slimming and classic, but also makes throwing together a funeral outfit a whiz.

MTV chic could be the
look for you if you weigh
in at less than 105 pounds,
frequent heavy metal
clubs, and don't mind
looking like a victime de
la mode.

*Cons:*

1. MTV chic can be hazardous to your health, since it's easy to catch cold in your underwear, and stiletto heals, like ancient Chinese foot binding, transform healthy feet into bunioned deformities, and are bad for your back.
2. Even minute specks of cellulite can look like giant craters under some lightweight spandex. It's unwise to even think of wearing it if you are more than ten ounces overweight.
3. Even incredibly fit older women look silly dressed like rockers, and *everybody* looks like they're trying much too hard and taking themselves much too seriously.
4. Bustiers and slip girdles are setting women's liberation back forty years.
5. Individuality takes a backseat to false nails.

Credits to: Madonna, Marisa Tomei, Carre Otis, Hell's Angels, *Rip* magazine, *Vogue,* and of course, MTV.

## *Le Sportif Motif*

Dressing like a jock is nothing new really; it's just become much more a part of legitimate fashion than it ever was before. When the look was still in its infancy in the late seventies and early eighties it was, no doubt, the most comfortable, unpretentious fashion approach of the century. You couldn't beat Reeboks and sweats. You could move, stretch, and easily ignore a few extra pounds. Everything could be tossed into the washer. Ironing was unnecessary. It was nirvana.

Today the look is a bit more affected. Workout clothes are color coordinated, layered, ride up the bum, and are as much of a pain to get in and out of as panty hose. And active sports–inspired fashions like bicycle shorts, stirrup ski pants, motorcycle jackets, and dresses shaped like wet suits seem a little bogus to me.

Decking yourself out in full sportif motif regalia can say two very different things depending on honesty of purpose. When it's the real thing—that is, the wearer actually *is* an active, healthy, sporty type—it says "I am strong, independent, and love enough about myself to keep this body in shape." When it's not real—say the wearer is immaculately coiffed, made-up, overmanicured, and looks like she never sweated a day in her life—the look, I'm afraid, once more smacks of victime de la mode.

Sportif motif—this ultimately sporty look is the peak of comfort and practicality, but tends to look just a wee bit affected when paired with an immaculately styled do and long painted nails.

*Pros:*

1. Seeing yourself in leotards and tights usually makes you want to eat less and exercise more.
2. Stirrup pants can be flattering since they tend to slim and lengthen the leg.
3. Leggings, which are derived from tights, are wonderfully comfortable and a boon to nineties' dressing.

4. Even when bicycle shorts go out of vogue tomorrow they can still be worn for riding bicycles.

*Cons:*

1. Bicycle shorts (while I'm on the subject) cut even the loveliest leg in half and are truly unflattering to anyone of any age, including tall lanky twenty-two-year-olds, on whom they look better, but still awful —especially when trimmed with lace. They should be fashion history by mid 1994, so save your money.

2. The wet suit belongs in the water where it was never particularly attractive, but was at least practical. Standout zippers and a form fit was a terrible idea for everyday fashions. I predict that wet suit–inspired designs will be history before I finish this sentence. Why would anyone want to copy wet suits? I don't get it.

Thank yous: Flo-Jo, Jane Fonda, Greg LeMond, Jacques Cousteau.

## Classic Chic

Classic chic, as I described it in my book, *Dressing Rich,* is dressing with simple elegance, class, and taste. It's sticking to the best of the classics and eshewing any style that smacks of trendy. Classic chic is neutral color schemes, natural fabrics (or excellent facsimiles), and simply styled garments that will be around forever. It is the timeless understated look of real class and money.

Classic chic can cost a lot of money if you go the haute route—lots of fabulous Armanis, Donna Karans, Calvins, etc. Or, once you've got the techniques down, you can pull it together on a relative shoestring.

Classic chic says "I am *innately* chic, elegant, and tasteful, and probably come from money. And I take care of myself and love looking marvelous, but it happens so naturally I really don't think about it much."

*Pros:*

1. You can go anywhere—with the exception of heavy metal clubs—and be treated with ultimate respect.

2. It's an easy look to dress down with inexpensive T-shirts, jeans, and sneakers.

3. Once your basic wardrobe is established you have to shop less—and spend less—to keep it current.

4. Since you stay within a limited color range almost everything you own will tend to mix and match—which makes life easy.

Classic chic—the look of elegance. Works best when topped with conscientious grooming and individual flair. Think Audrey Hepburn.

5. It is the perfect timeless boardroom look.
6. It's subtly monied without flash, which is the politically correct way to go.

*Cons:*

1. If you're the adventuresome, experimental, avant-garde, artsy type you could be bored by classy understatement. Classic chic is not on the cutting edge of fashion. Sorry, but that's the only drawback I can think of.

Thank yous: Jackie Kennedy Onassis, Audrey Hepburn, and even Fred Astaire.

## Yeeps (Young Environmentally Enlightened Professionals)

YEEPs are the nineties' variation of the seventies' preppies and the eighties yuppies. YEEPs are generally trim and healthy, since they have a penchant for healthy things like yoga and vegetarianism, and think organic. They do, however, tend to be on the pale side (unlike jocks) because, being environmentally attuned, they are fully aware of the dangers of the sun. They like natural fabrics and live in cottons and wools: cotton chinos or thin-wale cords, blue denim shirts, wool cardigans, loose cotton crewnecks. Loafers, desert boots, earth tones, and round horn-rimmed glasses all add to the look—comfortable, roomy, seriously concerned, practical, sensible, sturdy, well-scrubbed, no-nonsense, and casual. They are the personification of the Gap and J. Crew. Dyed-in-the-wool YEEPs try to buy from ethically correct companies that donate a percentage of their sales to the environment. And, needless to say, they all eschew fur like the plague (as well we all should).

YEEP dressing says "I'm serious, educated, evolved, environmentally aware, and maybe even rich. And, I appreciate fashion, but saving the whales is more important."

*Pros:*

1. Natural fibers are terrific. And supporting the environment is of benefit to all.
2. Almost everything you need for this look can be found in the J. Crew, Tweeds, Eddie Bauer, L. L. Bean, and Patagonia catalogs, so you never have to leave the house.
3. Clothes last a long time, so you get your money's worth.

*Cons:*

1. All those earth tones and muted colors can be depressing in gray weather.

Thank yous: the Gap and clones, Calvin Klein, Tommy Hilfiger, Ralph Lauren, and Katharine Hepburn.

There you have it—the major fashion trends of the nineties. Almost every picture you see in fashion magazines and almost all the clothing you find in the stores will be some variation on one of these themes, or a composite of a few of them. Now that you're fully in tune with all their fine points, and the psychological ramifications thereof, you're ready to discriminatingly pick and choose among them to shape an individual look that *says what you want it to say.*

Also, it's interesting to note that even though each of the preceding five looks takes its own unique approach to dressing, they all touch on a concept or two that we'll be incorporating into our overall *Dress Like a Million* plan: concepts like investment buying, recycling, quality, minimalism, uniform dressing, eclecticism, and comfort. But before we get into the actual nuts and bolts of that plan, it's important that we touch on the primary elements of fashion. These are the basics that every woman who dresses needs to know. Without this information fashion can be a mystery and a hassle. With it, it's a snap.

YEEPS—Preppie meets yuppie to become a more evolved and thankfully more environmentally conscious nineties' creature.

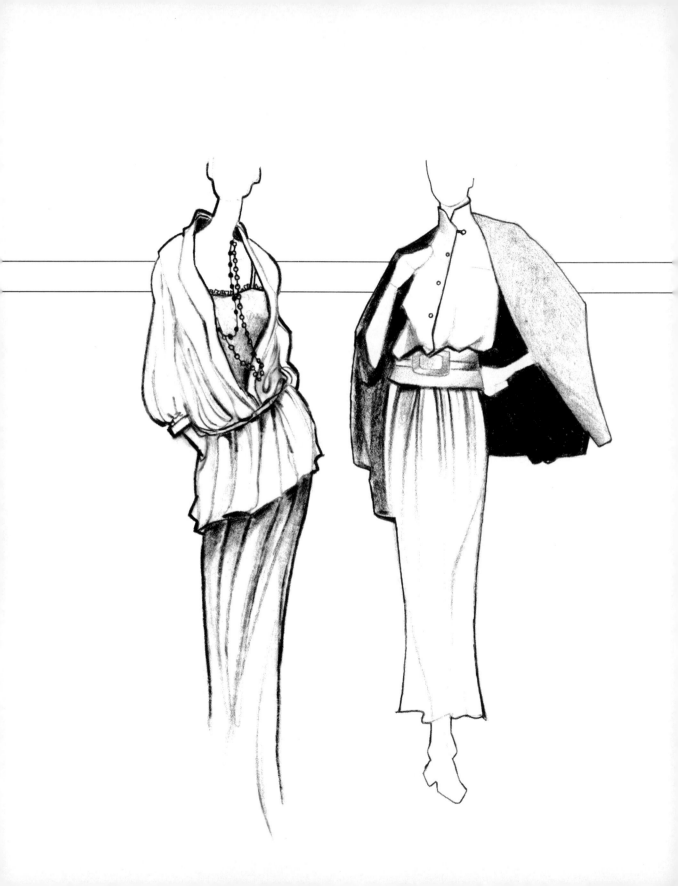

# CHAPTER 2

# Go Figure

## PROPORTION, LINE, AND DESIGN

Essentially every garment is made up of four major design components: proportion, line, color, and texture. For an outfit to score a perfect ten, each of those elements has to be in perfect harmony with the others—and, of course, with *you*. It's the "you" part that humanizes and, to a degree, complicates matters. If you weren't in the loop, fashion formulas could be as precise as rocket science. But since each of us is as different and unique as a snowflake, we have to consider all basic fashion information with our specific individual body proportions, coloring, personalities, tastes, and life-styles in mind.

## PROPORTIONS: THE UPS, DOWNS, HIGHS, AND LOWS

If you've ever wondered why your best friend looks better in a particular outfit than you do, or why some women look good in anything, or why slacks seem to suit you better than skirts, or why you love something in the store but it never seems right when you try to wear it the answer is probably *proportion*.

Proportion has a tremendous effect on your overall look. The better you can see it and the more you understand about it, the better you'll look— whether your couturier is Armani or army-navy.

*19*

Unlike color or texture, which are pretty obvious even to an untrained eye, proportion can be so subtle that it's easy to overlook. It's not unusual to hear someone remark "That's a great color," but how many times do you hear "Hey, love that proportion"? Not too often I wager. When you've got proportion working for you you're more likely to hear comments like "You look great" or "Did you lose weight?" or "You look younger." When proportion is working against you, you won't hear much at all.

Proportion is basically a simple matter of interdependent space-size relationships. Loosely translated into fashion terms that means that when one section of your body looks longer, wider, or larger, another section will appear shorter, narrower, or smaller. For example, a long jacket with large shoulder pads will make your torso appear longer and broader, which in turn will make your lower body appear shorter and smaller. It's that easy. When the proportions of your clothes are in harmony with the proportions of your body you've satisfied the first prerequisite of great fashion. When they're not, something will seem off. You might not be able to put your finger on it, but you simply won't look as good as you could.

In these days of anything-goes fashion, of course, it's perfectly acceptable *not* to look your best. Some days you might rather look funky than elegant. That's fine as long as it's a *conscious* decision. When you take a direct, "I'm off and I'm proud" approach you're operating in the realm of bas couture, which can be very hip and nineties or at least very California.

But let's not jump ahead of ourselves. Even successful dressing down calls for some solid proportional know-how. *You have to know the rules to break them with style.* Ill-suited fashion without the savvy to back it up moves out of the realm of attitude into the arena of bad taste or fashion victimhood, and neither is a particularly good look. And, anyway, in truth nobody really wants to look *bad;* some just want to look like they didn't try too hard.

Clothing silhouettes, of course, change with the times, and so do proportional ideals. In the classical Greek era, for instance, the silhouette was long, narrow, and flowing, and the ideal female stature was determined by multiplying the length of the head by seven and a half, which by my calculations, would make Dr. Ruth the embodiment of the perfect woman.

Today, fashion silhouettes cover the field—you can dress big one day in overlarge jeans and bulky sweater, slim the next in pencil pants and fitted jacket, or a combination of the two the day after. And proportional standards lean toward the tall and lanky, as epitomized by the world's top supermodels. So our proportional goals will be *overall balance* first and *elongation* second. Anyone who's rail thin and 5'8" or over can dismiss goal number two and concentrate on balance. The shorter and rounder you are the more important elongation becomes.

Proportion, though, is never just a matter of skinny or fat, short or tall. It's influenced by a slew of other variables: the placement of the waist, the length of the neck and legs, the shape of the shoulders, the width of the hips and waist, and the size and position of the bust. Even the distance between the armpit and the top of the shoulder varies from figure to figure.

In fact, it's my guess that that last particular variable helps Princess Di wear clothes so well. I just ran across an old magazine photo of her bikini-clad highness cruising the coast of Sardinia. And it seems to me that she measures an inch or so more than most of us from her armpit to the top of her shoulder. Without it I figure she'd be a bit more on the short-waisted side and would be more limited in her clothing styles. This is just a casual observance, of course; Di and I are not really that tight.

When it comes to bodies, the number of variations is staggering. All of us are built a little differently, and almost none of us are perfect. I'd guestimate that less than 10 percent of the entire female population has what could be termed a *perfectly proportioned body*. Years ago garment center mavens dubbed this enviable body type the "perfect $2.98 body," meaning that even their schlockiest, bottom-of-the-line $2.98 special would look good on it. Today they'd probably have to rename it the "perfect $202.98 body"—but we'll get into the fiscal fun of fashion later.

If you are one of the privileged and rare few with no proportional snags who can wear anything with impunity, God bless you—skip this chapter. As for the rest of you, take comfort in the fact that you're in excellent company. Even some of the world's great beauties are less than perfectly proportioned. Many of the models and actresses I've worked with over the years have joked about their "Stella d'Oro breadstick arms and legs," "flat derrieres," "chipmunk pouch ankles," ski-slope shoulders," "banana noses," and so on. They can joke about their problem areas because they've successfully figured out how to deal with them, and they realize they've got a lot of other things going for them. And so do you.

By understanding your particular proportions and using fashion to highlight your attributes and detract from your flaws you can look every bit as good as any of our lucky perfectly proportioned sisters—all seventeen or eighteen of them.

Whatever your shape or size, though, it's of upmost importance to accept and love yourself just the way you are. Forgive me if I sound like a new-age cheerleader here, but it's true. Dressing well starts with feeling good about

The perfectly proportioned body.

yourself. A heavyset friend of mine refers to her "weight *challenge*," never her weight *problem*, and reflects on how lucky she is to have great eyes, relatively small breasts, and a perfectly shaped head. Her glass is half full, not half empty. She concentrates on her assets and thinks positively. And I recommend that you do the same.

To truly understand your particular proportions, which is the necessary first step in choosing the right clothes, you have to assess your body realistically, but you don't have to be overcritical. If there's something you don't like about yourself—like your weight or muscle tone, for instance—take some positive action and change it. Exercise is free. But if you're obsessed about something that *can't be changed*—like height, wide hips, or heavy ankles—do yourself a favor and learn to love them. Obsession with the unalterable is detrimental to your health. Focusing on your attributes is not only smarter and healthier but also will put a smile on your face, which in the long run, makes for a better overall look. And if we are to believe a recent Brandeis University report, the nineties' notion of the perfect female form is genetically impossible for most women to achieve anyway. So give yourself a break.

The first thing you're going to need in order to take that initial no-holds-barred physical inventory—and to check proportion whenever you get dressed—is a good-quality full-length mirror. If you don't have one, get one. It's next to impossible to truly see proportion without it. If you do need to make the purchase, though, try to avoid those carnival distortion specials that reflect different images depending on where you stand. True, you might look like Cindy Crawford at times, but then just an inch to the left lurks the Michelin man. It's not worth the emotional turmoil.

### The Naked Truth

Once your mirror is in position you're going to have to strip down and take a good long look at the naked truth. The test here is to regard yourself as a saint would—totally nonjudgmentally. Remember, you are doing this to *objectively evaluate yourself* so you can use fashion effectively to disguise whatever flaws you find, not to mercilessly beat yourself up.

In case there's any doubt as to the difference, an evaluation might go something like this: "Ah yes, there is my body. I see I have an average length neck, slightly sloping shoulders, medium-sized breasts, wide hips, average legs, etc., etc." While the nonsaintly approach might sound something like this: "Oh my God, am I outta shape! I'm falling apart. My stomach is grotesque, my neck looks stubby, my boobs are saggy, I hate my knees. . . ." You get the idea. Go the saintly route. Please.

## *Figuring Out Your Proportions*

Since the body is the sum of its parts, which makes for countless proportional variations and combinations, it's impossible to categorize or classify body types as such. But I have noticed over the years that women's bodies

The Lily

The Orchid

The Rose

The Tulip

do tend to fall into four general categories, or *prototypical* body types, based on where extra weight settles—not that it necessarily *does* settle, of course, but if it did—hypothetically. See if you recognize any of these:

*The Lily:* Usually long and slender, the Lily tends to store extra weight in the waist, stomach, and sometimes the bust. The derriere is usually more flat than round. This body type looks totally at home riding to hounds.

*The Orchid:* A generally small slim frame that holds extra weight on the upper thighs and lower derriere, where it is oft referred to by the less poetic as "saddlebags."

*The Rose:* Lush, with a generous bosom and full hips, the Rose was Renoir's favorite model type. Extra weight is generally evenly distributed, though waists often remain slim. This type can be sexier out of clothes than in.

*The Tulip:* Tulips (aka pears) tend to have narrow shoulders, rib cages, and waists, and be broad and full on the bottom. Extra weight usually heads straight to the hips without passing Go. The best styles for tulips balance this discrepancy.

Even if you don't recognize yourself instantly in the preceding sketches, chances are you'll at least identify more strongly with one prototype than the others. The purpose here is to help you pinpoint any existing or potential problem areas as well as, of course, to remind you that we are all perfect flowers, no better or worse than the others, just different varieties. So find your prototype, study yourself in your trusty mirror, and then read on to discover your best lines and styles.

The main idea is to let your clothing reshape your "natural balance." Through the clever use of line, color, and texture you can create the look of a different proportion by accentuating your positive features and deemphasizing your negative ones. Let's examine *line* first.

## WHAT'S YOUR LINE?

One of the reasons certain outfits work better for you proportionately than others is *line*. Line is the basic silhouette or shape of an outfit, as well as the detailing (and/or fabric pattern) within a garment that creates spatial illusion. There are essentially four kinds of lines to watch for.

1. *Vertical* lines lengthen as they lead the eye up and down, making you appear taller and slimmer. Examples: deep V necks, shoulder-to-hem-line seams, and pleats. Single vertical lines give the greatest impression of height, which is why one color from shoulder to hem makes you look

Vertical lines

taller—it creates one unbroken vertical line. If there are a few vertical lines repeated at intervals across a garment, the elongating effect will be slightly diminished because the eye will tend to move horizontally as well as vertically.

2. *Horizontal* lines lead the eye from side to side, emphasing width making you appear heavier and shorter. Exception: You *can* get a somewhat lengthening effect if the horizontal line falls noticeably above or below the middle of your body, since it will then make either your torso or legs seem unusually long. So don't feel you have to chuck out all garments with horizontal lines in them, just those with lines in detrimental places like across the hips. And try not to let horizontals be the dominant lines in any particular outfit.

Horizontal lines

Diagonal lines

3. *Diagonal* lines lead the eye diagonally across the body, creating angles. The more vertical a diagonal line, the more lengthening it will be. The more horizontal, the more widening. When diagonal lines are used in a pair to form a V, the body will look narrower at the point where the lines meet, and wider where the V diverges.

4. *Curved* lines, whether in the form of draping, edges, or seaming, actually do the same thing as straight lines, but in a less obvious, softer, way. Since they tend to echo the curves of the body they make for a gentler, more feminine look.

Curved lines

Obviously some lines will be more flattering to your body than others. A full-bodied Rose, for instance, should think verticals or soft curved verticals to help balance her proportions, while a straight Lily could take advantage of the occasional horizontal line. Some lines are also better suited to particular personalities. Romantic feminine types, for example, generally lean toward curved lines, while very tailored types instinctively head for straighter, more geometric lines.

It's important to be aware of how particular lines work in relation to your body, and how they're used in particular designs. *The most sophisticated designs make optimum use of a minimum of lines*. Note, too, that certain lines might be compatible with your body in theory, but totally out of step with the general nineties' silhouette. A seventies' snug-bodiced Diane Von Furstenberg diagonal wrap dress, for instance, simply wouldn't cut the style muster today. Today's silhouette, while perhaps *slightly* less boxy and a tad more nipped-in than the eighties', is still simple, fluid, and comfortable.

There are a few *general* proportional tenets that seem to apply to most of us regardless of body shape. *Long over short, short over long* is one of the most basic. All that means, of course, is that a *long* jacket or top looks best with a *short* skirt, and a *short* jacket or top looks better with a *long* skirt. Another basic: the shorter the skirt, the lower the heel. (See Chapter 6.)

OK, enough theory, let's get down to specifics: *your* body and how you can best use line and proportion to your *individual* advantage. I'm going to assess the body part by part, noting particular variables. Read all the sections, but concentrate most on those that apply directly to you. We might as well start at the top.

## HEADS

There's absolutely nothing you can do to change the basic shape or size of your head—except, of course, to work with your coif. The standard school of thought is that your hairdo, should be in proportion with the rest of your body, both in length and volume. A big-volume Dolly Parton do, therefore, would technically be proportionately out of sync on a small slender woman. And likewise, a close-cropped gamine style would be risky on a large heavy woman.

Does that mean that small women should never go for volume or large women should avoid all close-cropped coifs? Yes, most of the time, but I never say never. As I will stress throughout this book there are always exceptions to every rule. My good friend Gayle, a size 14, clips her gray hair shorter than a rookie marine's—and looks great. Gayle says that she realized about fifteen years ago that she was always pulling her hair back and that she was "happiest not wearing my hear, but wearing my face." So Gayle, who's been in and around the fashion business for twenty years and knows herself extremely well, went full out and cultivated a strong, eccentric ultrashort style that has more or less become her signature. She likes to stand out and look different. She feels that she looks too ordinary with a common hairdo. The moral: When you have the know-how and are confident with your own personal style, you can make your own rules.

The important thing to keep in mind is that hair length and shape are a significant part of your entire fashion silhouette, which is why designers always consider the general hair motif for their models when showing a collection. If you have longish hair you've probably already noticed that it looks better pulled back with some outfits, pulled up with others, and worn down with yet others. So when you do your proportion check in your trusty mirror, don't forget your head (more on hair in Chapter 9).

*Tip:* In general, a small head makes the body below it look taller, just as a long neck creates the illusion of height.

## NECKS

Necks are not something we tend to think about (read "obsess over") as much as, say, hips or bust, but they do affect our overall proportions. Long slender necks are a fashion asset, since they allow many more style options —but not to worry if your neck is short to average.

### Short Necks

You can make your neck appear longer with vertical and/or diagonal lines. A basic V-necked shape, for instance, with or without lapels, creates a flattering line from below the chin to where the V converges. Since the eye tends to follow the line to the bottom of the V, the neck looks longer. Blouses worn open over a camisole, or even a V-necked T-shirt, give the same elongating effect.

A long string of *smallish* beads, some chains, or a long finely textured (never too bulky) oblong scarf left nonchalantly hanging loose or knotted low also creates a vertical line and adds length.

Watch too much hair hiding the neck. Short hair (in a good cut) can actually elongate the neck.

Avoid high collars or styles that fall *directly* on the neckline like jewel collars or top-buttoned blouses. They appear to abruptly separate the neck from the torso and therefore accentuate the shortness of the neck. Ditto for short choker necklaces.

Turtlenecks are even more risky, but it you love them for their practicality in cold climates and can't live without them, at least stay away from bulky ones and keep in mind that darker colors are more slimming—even on a neck. Also looser, shorter turtlenecks that can be scrunched down to show more of the neck are a better choice.

Long dangling earrings are generally risky, since they can focus attention exactly where you don't want it, but I have seen some nonchunky styles that swing and move with the body look quite good.

One of the biggest mistakes you can make is mega–shoulder pads. Standard size is fine, but if shoulder pads are too large all of a sudden your shoulders are up under your ears, and whatever little neck you started with totally disappears, making for a mini-linebacker look. This is a full-fledged, red-flagged, serious risk.

Deep V-necks like this one create a flattering vertical line that visually helps elongate a short neck.

Long necks provide lots of room for turtlenecks, cozy cowl necks, turned-up collars, or any combination thereof.

## Long Necks

Long necks instantly create the illusion of height, and as we've discussed, tall is in. So if you've got a lovely swanlike neck sitting on your shoulders count yourself blessed.

Here are some ways to take advantage of it:

Try a luxurious drapey cowl neck over a lightweight turtleneck—a great opportunity for an unexpected color or texture mix. Or a large man's tailored shirt worn over a roomy relaxed turtleneck. Don't forget to turn the collar up—you've got plenty of room.

Scarves are a natural. Try wrapping a long, soft silk or rayon one a few times around your neck—or even wear two together. (See Chapter 6.)

Sophisticated décolletage and other styles that bare neck and shoulders can be quite dramatic for evening.

Boat necks, with their horizontal line, are generally more flattering than scoop necks, which are in turn definitely more flattering than deep U necks.

Any length hair works with a long neck, but if hair is cut short, best to keep it long enough in back to cover the nape of the neck.

And, of course, there's lots of room for jewelry.

## SHOULDERS

Your shoulders will be either broad, narrow, sloping, or average. Shoulder shape and width is an important variable, since it has a tremendous effect on the way a garment drapes on your frame.

### Square Broad Shoulders

These are definitely more of a fashion plus, since, like a good hanger, they give clothes a nice solid base from which to hang and drape. If, however, you feel your shoulders are proportionately *too* broad, simply stay away from horizontal lines on top and anything that visually squares the shoulders like square necklines and obviously set-in sleeves.

*Other tips:*
- Try V necks or leaving shirt collars open to create a vertical line that will counteract the broad horizontal of the shoulders.
- Make sure to remove shoulder pads from all garments.
- Avoid extended-shoulder styles (epaulets are not for you) and bulky fabrics.
- Consider styles that drape gently over the shoulders like dolman, raglan, or kimono sleeves.
- Wear camisoles and tank tops with straps that fall closer to the neck than to the edge of the shoulders.
- Wear baggy trousers, gathered skirts, or other styles that will add a bit of dimension below if you're slim through the hips.

### Narrow Shoulders

If you're narrow all over, these are rarely a problem. If, however, like a Tulip, you're narrower on the top than bottom, you need to balance the proportional discrepancy. Shoulder pads are a godsend because they allow clothes to fall and drape straight down from their extended breadth. In fact, one tulip-shaped friend of mine finds shoulder pads so indispensable that she jokes they should be the next surgical implant. *Everyone with narrow or sloping shoulders needs shoulder pads.* Experiment until you find the perfect shapes for you, and always have a ready supply in dark and light colors.

*Other tips:*
- Consider boat necks because they create a horizontal line across the shoulders that gives the illusion of width.
- Stick to roomier tops. Tight tops automatically make the hips look larger.
- Wear monotone outfits—they also help equalize top and bottom.

## *Sloping Shoulders*

All the above narrow-shoulder advice holds. The basic idea: Square off the shoulders. Shoulder pads with nice squared-off blunt edges should be a wardrobe mainstay.

*Other tips:*

- Choose set-in and extended shoulders.
- Keep shoulders covered.
- Avoid oversized neck bows, ascots, or heavy necklaces or other jewelry since these only accentuate the narrowness of the shoulders.
- Choose dolman or raglan sleeves carefully (superrisky since these drape and follow the natural line of the shoulder)—but even they can work over those trusty shoulder pads.

## BUSTS

### *Large*

Big breasts have made a bit of a comeback this decade. Models, you'll note, are much curvier than they were in the seventies and early eighties. So if you're full bosomed you will be thrilled to know that you are officially in vogue (at least for the moment). If you're tall and long to average waisted, your big bust won't be much of a fashion problem because your torso is proportionately long enough to accommodate the extra dimension.

But if you're short and/or short waisted, a big bust tends to dominate the whole upper part of your body and throws proportions slightly out of kilter. In that case, look for bras that create the greatest waist to bust separation. Minimizer bras offer maximum support, control, and shape, and since they gently push the breasts to the side rather than to the front, they can reduce visual breast size by up to two inches.

*Other tips:*

- Avoid wide belts—you don't want your bosom perched atop a piece of leather—and other styles that shorten the torso.
- Think roomy simple designs—tight-fitting garments only accentuate what's under them.
- Wear monochromatic outfits—a definite best bet, since they present an overall impression. The more you break up the body with color the more noticeable each individual part becomes.
- Lower your waistline by draping a soft, fluid top over a thin belt worn on your hips to add extra inches above the waist and make the bustline less obvious.

- Stay away from bulky fabrics. Think fluid silks, rayons, and unlined garments.
- Don't wear pins, hanging pendants, or other jewelry on your bust. Try a stickpin or brooch on your jacket lapel. If you do like hanging pendants—or little bottles or what have you—look for flat ones. Nothing big and chunky.
- Use jackets as great camouflagers—they counteract your curves with geometric lines. Slightly boxy shapes are usually more flattering than fitted styles—especially if you are full through the hips. The trick is finding great designs in soft fluid fabrics like washed silks (see Chapter 4) that sort of float around your body. Perfect jackets can cost you, but they are one of the best investment buys going.
- Avoid excess detailing around the bust like patch pockets, piping, yokes, etc.
- Think vertical lines above the waist. V necks, shawl collars, and open collars work well. Stay away from horizontal lines.
- Watch your posture. A lot of women who blossom early develop a bad habit of slouching slightly to hide their largesse—plus there's the pull of the extra weight. If you're extralarge and suffering any kind of major discomfort, you might want to consider consulting a doctor about the possibility of a breast reduction, since you could be at risk for serious back problems down the road.

### Small

Small busts present relatively few proportional problems, since it's always easier to add visual dimension than to subtract it. My basic advice: Count your blessings; small breasts hold up best over the long haul. If, however, you don't want to call attention to the fact that you have small breasts simply stay away from anything tight fitting. Think loose roomy tops, layers, and pleats.

Under very bulky fabrics you might consider a fiberfill contour bra that can add a little extra shape. If you're an extreme Tulip body type, that is, very heavy on the bottom and small on top, you could even wear slightly padded bras to help balance proportion.

But, please, just because the magazines are showing bustier models does not mean you have to have to run out and get breast implants to keep up with the times. There are too many horror stories out there to even think twice about them, unless you need them for reconstruction or are *seriously* psychologically troubled about your breast size. The potential health dangers far outweigh any cosmically inconsequential fashion whims.

## *High and Low*

Take note of your bust placement. Is it exceptionally low or high? If your breasts are high, strapless-type gowns and/or halters may look a little strange because there will be relatively little expanse of skin between the top of the halter and the chin. If your bust is large and unusually low, consider underwire bras, which create the greatest space between bust and waist, and avoid wide belts and other styles that focus attention on the problem area.

## WAISTS

Waists come in four varieties: small, thick, long and short.

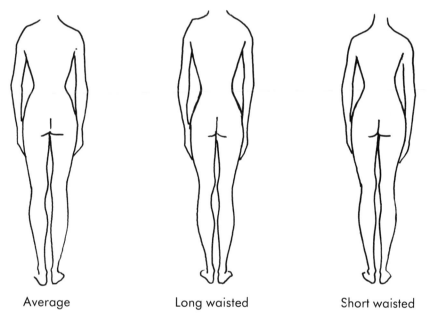

| Average | Long waisted | Short waisted |

The easiest way to tell if you're long or short waisted is to look at your naked backside in a full-length mirror.

*Small* waists have been a universally accepted fashion plus way before Scarlett O'Hara obsessed about hers. So if you have one play it up with interesting belts, dresses that can be nipped in at the waist, and slacks and skirts with well-defined waistlines. There's only one drawback I can think of when it comes to a small waist and that's when it's paired with ample hips like our prototype Rose. In that case if you nip in the waist too tightly the hips will appear larger—and it might not be worth the trade-off.

*Thick* waistlines are much less of a figure problem these days because of the profusion of oversize tops, jackets, and loose-waisted dresses. The basic idea, of course, is to wear garments that are not defined at the waist or that help mask the width, such as vests, overshirts, cardigans, and jackets. Blouson styles are another perfect foil; try belting below the natural waistline and draping a bit over the top of it. When belts show, keep them the same color as your outfit and avoid flashy buckles.

If you're thin to average, a wide elastic belt worn with the bottom of the belt below your natural waistline visually lowers a high waistline.

The *long* and *short waist* variable has much more of an impact on the way clothes fit and is a lot trickier to deal with—and to spot. To ascertain whether your waist is long, short, or average, turn up the heat (or do this exercise in summer), strip down to your birthday suit, turn your back to your full-length mirror, and spy on yourself with a hand or compact mirror.

If you are *short waisted,* the distance from your waist indentation to the bottom of your buttocks will look longer than the distance from your waist indentation to your armpits.

If you are *long waisted,* the opposite will be true; the distance from your waist indentation to your armpits will be longer than the distance from waist indentation to the bottom of your buttocks.

If you are *average,* these distances will be just about equal.

Now that you know what you are, the question is what do you do about it.

## Short Waisted

Let's look at the short-waisted variable first since I live with that one every day and know it all too well.

A *short waist* usually means relatively long legs—that's the good news. So the trick is to preserve the long-legged look while at the same time making the torso look longer—or at least not any shorter. Since we just discussed what lines can do, one obvious solution would be to use vertical lines to elongate the torso. A blouse worn open to the waist over some sort of camisole, for instance, would create vertical lines.

Also . . .

- Belts are a natural since they are like movable waistlines. Technically if you drop a belt *below* the natural waist the torso will appear longer. While that does indeed work in theory, you also have to consider the size of your hips. If they are generous you probably wouldn't want to highlight them by slinging a belt across them. If, on the other hand, you keep the entire outfit one color, and blouson a roomy top over the belt a tad, it could work.

  Belts that are the same color as your top will add visual inches to the torso. And if you're relatively thin, wide *elastic* belts are terrific because they are pliable enough to be worn very low on the waist—the bottom half of the belt actually *below* your waistline. Then when you drape your top over the belt in a blouson fashion your waist appears to be at the bottom of the belt.

- A lot of slip and camisole straps will be too long. Camisoles with ajustable or spaghetti straps are easiest to fix. Also, full slips tend to look sexier than half slips.
- Monotone outfits, in general, make waistlines less noticeable.
- Watch jacket and tunic or overshirt lengths. Technically speaking, the shorter a top is the longer the legs will look, and the longer the top, the shorter the legs will look. So to keep your leg length don't wear tunics, overshirts, and jackets too long.

  To get the length right on any kind of top you always have to consider what you wear with them—it makes a big difference. Picture a gorgeous cream-colored, wood gabardine Armani-type suit with a *long-ish* jacket and a *short* skirt, for example. Worn together they are the perfect proportion (long over short). If you wore the cream jacket with black slacks it would probably look *too* long because the vertical line created by one overall color would be broken. And if you paired the jacket with a longer skirt, the jacket would most likely need to be shortened to balance the proportion (short over long). So always consider the colors and shapes of the bottoms you plan to wear with your jackets and overshirts.
- Also, even if shorter jackets make a temporary comeback (by definition all comebacks are temporary) and you decide to shorten any of your jackets, don't go overboard. An inch or less is often all that's needed to make a proportional shift.

  *Note:* If you wear a lot of tunic-type tops keep your jackets long enough to cover them.
- Slacks usually look terrific on long legs. If you find certain styles *too* high-waisted, try lowering the belt loops (or removing them altogether) and wearing your belt *below* the waistband. You can also find this style ready-made in the stores. Even though the top of the pants *is* still high, belting a few inches lower actually makes the waist appear lower. Try it, you'll see.
- Skirts (and slacks) designed *without* waistbands almost always work well.

### Long Waisted

There are probably more advantages than drawbacks to being slightly long waisted. You have more space above the waist for layering, wide, interesting belts can be worn at the natural waistline or popped over tunics, and dresses and skirts are usually easier to fit. All in all, it's an easy proportion to deal with. The longer your waist, though, the shorter your legs appear.

So consider these tips for longer looking legs:

What you wear with your jackets and overblouses makes a big difference proportionately. This jacket works better with a short skirt of the same color than with slacks of a contrasting color, since the elongating line created by one single color is broken.

- Skirts—especially long skirts—are usually proportionately easier to deal with than slacks, since you don't really notice where the legs begin. Ultrashort skirts tend to look even shorter on short legs since there is less material and less leg being covered. So watch microminis.
- When it comes to slacks go for high-rise or high-waisted styles and totally avoid any styles that even vaguely resemble hip huggers, such

as some men's jeans. Also forgo any styles that are full through the hips and taper down to the ankle, since they also accent the shortness of the leg. Cuffs are not a great idea either.

The best length for pants is long—to the instep of your shoe. If you do opt for ankle length be sure to balance proportion with a high waist and/or slim fit.

- Monotones (again) are a best bet, since they make waistlines less distinguishable, and the eye won't initially discern where the leg begins. Color and silhouette will be the focal points.
- Belts the same color as skirt or slacks can add extra inches to the legs.
- Tops with horizontal necklines or detailing will also help counterbalance torso length.

## BUTTOCKS, HIPS, AND THIGHS

If your hips, buttocks, and thighs are slim you can declare this area problem free and move on to the next section.

If you're heavy in these areas, read on but don't worry about it—these are the most common trouble spots for most women. Luckily, these days there are a lot of fashion remedies.

The basic strategy is to draw attention *away* from trouble spots and *toward* your more alluring features. So *keep things simple in the problem area.* That means forget about flowery printed slacks and polka-dot skirts.

- Dark neutrals are a great foil. Black, of course, being the number-one slimming color of all time. If you do opt for lighter colors, you're better off sticking to overall monotones. Again the reasoning is that if you visually divide your body with colors, each part will be noticed separately, whereas one color makes one overall impression.
- Monotone outfits with some attention-getting accessory near the face are especially effective, since this ploy will lead an admiring eye straight to your face where your effervescent personality can take over.
- Shoulder pads will help balance the proportional discrepancy between a small top and a broad bottom.
- Need I say it—never wear tight pants. This is a red-flag risk. Nothing makes bulges more obvious except maybe gluing a blinking light to your derriere. If you're very hippy I would suggest staying away from slacks and going the skirt and dress route.
- However, a loose, roomy overblouse or layered T-shirts, worn over black leggings or slim pants can work surprisingly well on some heavy-

hipped women. The trick is to make sure the big top hangs gracefully from the shoulders (or shoulder pads) and just skims the body—not clinging anywhere.

*Tip:* I've seen some great oversized overblouses at Lane Bryant.

• Stay away from skirts that are gathered all around or are pleated at the waist. A slight A-line is usually flattering, although a straight skirt made out of a substantial weight fabric is generally a better line with blazers.

• Another possibility: Try soft longish skirts that lie flat and snug over the hips and stomach, then layer a soft overblouse and even a vest or jacket over that. This look works best, again, in monotones.

*Tip:* If you can't find skirts that lie flat over belly and hips, consider having a tailor or dressmaker add a stretch cotton panel to the top of regular skirts.

• Jackets are great—if they're the right style. Short fitted jackets are, of course, the very worst choice, since they will accentuate a full bottom. Roomy, unconstructed jackets or even blazers are best bets—just watch the length and proportion. If jackets are too long, legs will look shorter. (See jacket section in Chapter 5.)

## STOMACHS

A flat one obviously is no problem. If yours is the protruding kind, stay away from belts and anything bulky around the waist. Big tops that cover but don't cling to the belly are naturals. Dark monotones, again, are winners. And skirts are usually an easier fit than pants (except for leggings which can be covered up with overblouses).

## LEGS

We've already discussed the pros and cons of long and short legs in the long-waisted/short-waisted section. But legs can also be skinny or heavy.

### Skinny Legs

These are less of a fashion problem than heavy ones, although I didn't necessarily think so when they called me bird-legs all through high school. The most problematic thing about ultraskinny legs is hem lengths. An inch or two in either direction can make the difference between legs looking

Soft-flowing long tops worn over snug-topped soft skirts of the same color can be a very flattering look.

semishapely or like toothpicks. The only way to discover the perfect hem length is to experiment. Try on one of your longest skirts, get in front of your full-length mirror, and keep rolling up the waist until you find the most flattering length for your legs. That at least will give you a range to work in. Then, of course, you'll have to take shoes and the rest of each particular outfit into consideration. I personally find shorter skirts (and even shorter Bermuda shorts) more flattering. But at this point in my life I've frankly accepted the fact that my legs are anemic and just let them look as skinny as they want to. It's my antifashion-proportion statement.

## Heavy Legs
Again, keep it simple in the leg area and draw attention elsewhere.

- Heavy legs are easily camouflaged with longish skirts and good weight, straight-legged trousers.
- Beware of flowing pajama-type pants that might seem like a good idea but tend to cling and actually accentuate the thigh when you move.
- *Black* leggings can work if the leg is shapely below the knee and thighs are partially covered by a great overblouse.
- Miniskirts are highly inadvisable.
- Watch heel heights and shapes. We all know that high heels, uncomfortable though they may be for some of us, do lengthen the leg, but a *very* narrow stiletto heel may look too delicate and ill proportioned with a heavy leg. Big clunky heels would be equally unattractive, since they would visually add extra weight to the leg. For dress, heels that are mid-height with a narrowish but not needle-thin heel would be a good starting point.

And here's one last interesting proportional tidbit about legs: If your legs are disproportionately longer above the knee (like mine) or very short below the knee, hem lengths are a little trickier. A skirt worn just below the knee can look too long because the distance between the waistline and the hem is out of proportion with the length of leg showing. So a lot more thought has to be given to the proportion of your top garments (jackets, sweaters, etc.). There's always more proportional adjustments to consider—another reason I find slacks easier and less of a hassle to wear.

You definitely need a little practice to be able to spot these kinds of proportional subtleties, but once you're aware of them and how they're created, you're way ahead of the game. To further train your eye study store windows, fashion magazines, and even people on the street. Make a game of trying to figure out why some outfits look balanced and why some don't—

a sort of fashion Trivial Pursuit, if you will. And definitely practice and experiment in front of your mirror. Try different hem lengths, clothing combinations, accessories, etc. Watch the way the focal points and silhouettes change and how different lines affect your body shape. Before long your proportional awareness will be second nature.

## EXTRA TIPS FOR SHORT WOMEN (5'3" AND UNDER)

In general all the preceding proportion variables information holds true, but there are just a few additional points. The most important thing to remember is that when you're small of stature you have a smaller fashion canvas to deal with. That is, you have less actual physical space to cover with clothing and accessories. So you really have to keep your fashion relatively uncomplicated and avoid clutter. Details like lapels, prints, pockets, etc. also have to be on a smaller scale so they don't overpower. Fabrics shouldn't be overly bulky and hair shouldn't be too long. Think neat, trim, simple, linear design.

Also, it's even more crucial that you stay fit and trim, since there is less room for extra weight to distribute itself. The truth is it's tougher for a short heavy woman to look chic than a heavy average-sized woman. It's not fair, but there it is.

# Color Ploys

## THE MINIMALIST APPROACH

By now everyone even semi-interested in fashion has heard of one color theory or another. While the terms vary somewhat, they all pretty much say the same thing: Choose colors that are most compatible with your skin tone, hair color, and personality. All true, and naturally we'll address those specifics here. But the nineties call for a few additional considerations as well. This decade we need colors that are also versatile, make our lives simpler, offer fashion longevity, and help us create a truly individual style. So all things considered, color choice today requires a bit more practicality and a little less cloth draping and color swatch shuffling.

The biggest favor you can do yourself in this no-nonsense decade is to *pare down* and *fine-tune your color palette*. Unless you have unlimited funds and a personal shopper, it simply takes too much time and money to deal with a lot of colors. So forget about incorporating all "your thirty special colors" into your wardrobe. The truth of the matter is that most of us look our best in five or six colors—seven, tops. You *can* wear others, but you won't look as good in those as you do in the initial lot, so why spread yourself all over the color chart?

If you want to test this theory for yourself, turn on the television and watch your favorite local female newscaster for a few weeks in a row. She'll probably wear her best four or five colors and look fabulous. Then, either because she gets bored or feels she owes her viewers a little variety, she'll slip in a few other colors, and, no surprise, the bloom's off the rose. She'll look washed out or less sparkly or more sallow. Same makeup, same lighting —questionable colors. Check it out for yourself. It's fun, semieducational, and cheaper than a movie. Note: If your favorite newscaster has suddenly developed unexpected fashion savvy, watch one on a different channel.

It becomes eminently clear just how thoroughly nineties a pared-down color palette is when you check off the advantages:

- You need fewer major accessories like shoes, boots, and handbags because the few good ones you acquire will go with everything.
- Shopping becomes easier and less time consuming, since you can zip through stores focusing on just a few colors while ignoring the rest.
- Getting dressed takes less time since almost everything mixes and matches.
- Wardrobe possibilities are actually extended, since everything goes so well together.

One of the surest ways to get the most from a minimalist color approach is to *use one or two neutrals for the basic foundation of your wardrobe* (i.e., jackets, skirts, slacks, coats), and then *add interest and dimension with two to six secondary or accent colors*. Ideally, your accent colors will be as complementary to each other as they are to your base neutral.

Since I've been dressing this way for years I can vouch for its effectiveness. I personally use black and white as my neutrals and add zip with with red, turquoise, royal blue, and varying shades of periwinkle. In the summer I lean more toward white and occasionally indulge in a touch of pink . . . and, OK, I *do* own a few pairs of khaki shorts (which look crisp and clean with white), but that's it for me. All my colors work well collectively: Black and white together is a timeless classic, and all the accent colors look great with black or white or with each other. Because I've been wearing these same colors for years, and gravitate toward easy, timeless classic styles, my wardrobe has gradually built upon itself to the point where I now need only add an occasional piece to stay current. The upshot: less shopping, more savings, more nineties.

According to color pundits I can theoretically wear green, lemon yellow, fuchsia, burgundy, gray, and a slew of other colors, but since they look terminally mediocre on me and would only complicate my life, I can think of no reason to clutter my closet with them. The less I have to think when I get dressed, the better I like it.

It's not surprising that all the fashion-savvy women I interviewed for this book agree that fewer colors translate into easy chic. But what *is* somewhat surprising is how many of these women, all of whom have very different shapes and coloring, have chosen black for their basic wardrobe neutral.

Actress Erin Grey calls herself "pretty much a black-and-white person," and raves about how much cheaper and easier it is to dress that way.

New York restaurateur ex-model Barbara Smith loves black because her style revolves around her jewelry, and she finds black "a great backdrop."

Actress-producer Deborah Raffin laughs when she notes, "You walk into my closet and it's all black or cream." Every once in a while, she says, "I'll shock someone and actually wear color. . . . for me it's the ultimate comfort not to have to think too much about what I put on."

Retail executive Gayle Shulman says, "I almost only wear black and white clothes. I wear black all year-round because it's flattering, and it's a lifesaver when I don't know what to wear. If I'm feeling especially uncomfortable at period time I can't imagine putting anything else on. And it suits me. It looks good with my coloring and my hair, and I almost always feel better wearing it—with rare exceptions."

And L.A. boutique owner Tracey Ross, who certainly has more access to more diverse fashions than most of us will in a lifetime, sees black as a perfect antidote to the ostentatious flash of the eighties, as well as an incredibly reliable standby. "It's just a classic, classic look," she says. "When I don't know what to wear and I want to look good, I always wear all black. I have so many clothes in my closet it's obnoxious, but I always end up wearing black. It's so easy—for travel too."

Although black *is* undoubtedly the easiest color on the planet to work with (see Chapter 5), it still may not be the perfect neutral for you. It can be draining to some very pale skin tones, and some blithe spirits may simply find it a bit too somber. Luckily, however, there are plenty of other fine neutral colors to choose from that are almost as versatile and that offer enough varieties of shades and tones to complement every complexion. Gray, beige, navy, tan, taupe, deep rich brown, and even grayish olive green are other fashion perennials that can be worn year after year and make wonderfully sophisticated color combinations. Aside from their versatility, these colors are also classically elegant, always tasteful, and trend resistant.

So choose a base neutral color (or colors) that feels comfortable and is most flattering to your personal coloring. Pale blondes might consider the beiges (from ivory to taupe to greige), aubergine, or navy. Any of the subtle, rich earth tones generally work well for women with auburn hair. Redheads and strawberry blondes almost always look great in slate blue, charcoal gray, and dusty sage. And black, navy, and white are best bets for dark brunettes and/or olive-skinned women.

These, of course, are just general suggestions. If you were one of the thousands of women who had a color chart done in the eighties—and still know where it is—scan your chart to see which *neutrals* your color consultant suggested. Then pinpoint the one or two that have served you best over the years and concentrate on them.

If you managed to avoid the color-chart rage, check through your closet and see which neutrals turn up most. You may have already subconsciously selected your base neutral. If not, try on some of the suggestions here when you go shopping. Pick the one that would go best with your favorite accent colors and that adds a glow to your skin. As the late Diana Vreeland once told me, "A color that's good for the skin is good for you. . . . You want colors that clear the skin and makes you feel warm towards yourself."

If you opt for more than one base neutral color *make sure the colors are totally complementary* and blend well with each other. If they don't harmonize and work together well, you'll be missing half the advantages of this efficient plan. So with the exception of combinations like black and white or navy and cream, it's a good idea to keep base neutrals in the same family. Dove gray and medium charcoal gray, for example, are good base colors in the same family. If you mixed and matched them, and accented with a touch of muted coral or cadet blue or red or even another shade of gray you'd have some very sophisticated color schemes happening. Most of the beiges, like taupe, greige, and sand, also look wonderful when combined.

You definitely have more options when it comes to choosing your accent colors, but if you want to add chic to your wardrobe as well as a dash of color, make sure your small selection includes a few muted tones. Pastels especially look more sophisticated in slightly grayed-down tones. A subtle slate blue, for example, would win hands down in terms of chic over pure baby blue, and there'd be no contest between a dusty rose and raucous bubble-gum pink.

Bright colors have their place too, especially red—an extraordinarily effective color that looks terrific with almost all of the recommended neutrals (beige, tan, gray, green, navy, black, white, etc.) and with most skin tones. In fact, it goes so well with so many colors that I sometimes—only half jokingly—refer to it as "the neutral of the nineties" even though it is technically more aggressive than a classic neutral.

Bright colors make such an appreciable statement of their own, though, that it's best to limit them to the occasional sweater, blouse, or accessory—especially if you are on a particularly tight budget. Here's why:

1. They will definitely be remembered more than subtler shades, which means you will probably end up wearing them less—and therefore getting less mileage from them.

2. Since details are more noticeable on brightly colored clothes, pieces have to be fairly well constructed to look decent—which almost always translates into higher cost.

3. Brightly colored garments have to be *especially well suited* to the individual lest they look loud, flashy, and/or tacky.

4. They're less mood versatile. Since you *will* be noticed in brights— especially an outfit made up of *predominantly* bright colors—they're really better suited for your cheerier, outgoing days than your shy retiring ones. Again—less mileage.

All accent colors, though, brights included, can come in handy when you want to refocus attention. They can act as a sort of focal spotlight leading the eye away from a negative straight to a positive. If, for instance, you've got knockout blue eyes, wearing a similar color near your face would make them even more striking.

Some colors, on the other hand—such as mustard, bright fuchsia, chartreuse, and pure orange—simply look awful on everyone regardless of eye, hair, or skin color. And I'm sorry, but I will never understand camel. It never fails to amaze me that some people actually consider it an elegant color when it does *absolutely nothing* for *anybody*. It saps the color right out of men, women, and children, fair, ruddy, or dark. In that sense, I guess, it has earned its place in fashion—as a great equalizer.

Once you've chosen your neutrals and accent colors the main thing to consider is *balance*. Good fashion, like fine art, requires top-notch composition. The most goof-proof balance method is dressing in one overall color— with or without slight variations in tone. Monochromatic outfits (in the suggested neutrals) always look chic, especially when made up of interesting textures, and also have the advantage of producing such a unity of color that the total impression becomes stronger than the individual parts of your outfit. That means you can get by with some less expensive pieces. If, for instance, you put together an all beige outfit with a jacket, skirt, silk blouse, and long charmeuse silk scarf, the blouse could be medium priced since it would blend in so well with the rest of the ensemble as to be practically unnoticed. If you wore the same blouse with, say, a black jacket, it would be much more obvious and have to be more of a gem.

Another easy way to assure balance—and this is more goof *resistant* than goof *proof*—is simply to *keep your base neutral dominant,* that is, let it constitute the majority of a particular outfit's color, then add any desired pizzazz with your second neutral and/or your choice of accent colors. You would have to work overtime to upset the balance in an outfit that was 70 to 75 percent one color. If, for instance, your trousers (or skirt) and jacket were black (or *your* neutral), the outfit would, in most cases, maintain its equilibrium regardless of what colors you added in the form of a blouse, scarf, bracelets, or what have you. You could, of course, choose *unattractive* colors, but it would be difficult to choose *compositionally* wrong colors. Yes, shiny white patent leather shoes *would be* a formidable mistake, but that's what I mean by "working overtime."

You also can't go too wrong mixing colors of the same *value* (value is the lightness or darkness of a color), especially when, again, you keep one color dominant. I used to work with a TV cameraman who always dressed marvelously in very unusual and adventurous shades of muted pastels. I thought he had great color sense. As it turned out he was almost totally color blind and chose his colors by their value alone. Like I said, it's hard to go too wrong.

Very subtle value blends make for wonderfully sophisticated color combinations. Imagine, for example, how chic classic gray flannel would look with a dark dusty lilac, muted sage, or antique turquoise. One way to check values is to simply squint your eyes. Through squinted eyes like-valued colors look almost the same. In fact, in black and white photos they will look almost identical. Tan and red, navy and deep green, and charcoal and deep periwinkle are other interesting possible like-value color mixes.

Where you do have to pay particular attention to balance is when mixing strong contrasting colors, i.e., very pale shades with very deep shades. In that case it generally works better to keep the darker tones on the bottom for three reasons: (1) Lighter and/or brighter colors draw the eye first, and it's better to make your first impression with your face rather than your knees. (2) Darker shades are regressive and therefore tend to be more slimming—and slim hips are a figure plus in our society. (3) Darker shades on the bottom tend to lend the figure a certain stability. The closer your colors are in value, of course, the less you have to worry about this.

If for whatever reasons you do opt to wear lighter shades on the bottom, at least consider balancing them with a little something light on top. Say you're wearing white pants with a navy blouse, you could let a white camisole or T-shirt peak out from under the blouse, or even wear the navy blouse *over* a white blouse with a similarly shaped collar, creating, in effect, a double-collared blouse. You could also, of course, create a balance with jewelry, a scarf, or a shawl.

*Reminder:* Extreme color contrasts tend to visually break up the body and add girth. So if you're heavier on the bottom than you would ideally like to be, you're better off sticking to one allover color or mixing colors of the same value, since that will make you look slimmer.

When mixing strong contrasting colors it usually works best to keep darker colors on the bottom. But if you do opt for lighter colors below, think about balancing with a touch of the light color on top. This double blouse combo works like a charm.

## PLAIDS, PRINTS, AND PATTERNS:

Plaids, prints, stripes, and other patterns actually play a rather minor role in a select pared-down nineties' wardrobe; they become more of an accessory than an essential part of your wardrobe. I should note that when I first started this book most of the fashion magazines were touting plaids as the latest and greatest thing to come down the chute. But now as we're going to press the plaid craze has already run its course. A lesson in trends right there.

The problem with most patterns is that they're self-limiting. They're too noticeable and go with too few other garments to be worn a lot and are nearly impossible to update with accessories. So they're not worth a heavy investment. That's not to say rule them out altogether; simply don't spend major dollars on them. Even something as seemingly classic as a plaid Chanel (or Chanel-style) suit misses when you compare it with a classic solid Armani (or Armani-type) suit. The solid Armani jacket could go from board-walk (with T-shirt) to boardroom (with silk) in a flash—for years. The Chanel would be more easily dated, and although I have seen jackets from Chanel-type suits paired with other skirts, slacks, and jeans, they never look quite right.

Plaid or small-patterned jackets and/or suits are something to think about *after* you've got your basic wardrobe up and running, not before. One of the few exceptions I can think of is a comfy, understated tweed jacket that blends magnificently with almost all your chosen colors. In that case you'd probably get quite a lot of wear out of it.

As accessories and relatively *inexpensive* wardrobe additions, though, patterns, prints, and plaids are definite contenders. Just keep them simple; the greater the subtlety, the greater the longevity. Unless you live on a tropical island or are related to Dorothy Lamour, big splashy prints simply aren't happening anymore—except as a lark. They're too silly for the nineties. Small floral patterns can be lovely for light summer skirts and dresses, and plaids are great in the form of classic flannel shirts, scarves, and shawls, and, as I mentioned, *understated* tweed slacks or jackets.

Also—and I hate to bring this up—there's an age thing. As you get older you really don't need a lot of loud, busy, stripes, lines, and swirls competing for attention. You want colors and fabrics that will soften any lines or wrinkles, not echo and accentuate them. Leave the loud stuff to the teen-agers.

Obviously whatever plaids, patterns, and prints you do incorporate into your wardrobe should fit comfortably into your small color family. Then, aside from tossing on the occasional print shirt now and then, you could really get creative and mix and match patterns like the pros. Since you're already in the same color family, all you have to remember is that one pattern should be predominant. You could even successfully mix as many as three separate patterns: say, a pair of subtly *plaid* flannel slacks, with a quiet *argyle* sweater vest, and a long *striped* scarf, as long as you stay within your color family and keep one of the patterns more important than the others.

The next time you're thumbing through a fashion magazine, study the way some of the designers put together various patterns. Some of them, like Ungaro, come up with ingenious combinations that will definitely tweak your imagination.

And, lastly, remember that whether you're dealing with solids or patterns the colors you wear create immediate impressions that will affect even the fashion unaware. Pure pastels, for instance, are a lot more girlish and naive than serious, sexy black, which in turn is less dynamic and passionate than fiery red. The more subtle your colors and color combinations the less aware people will be of the influence color has on them, but they will be affected whether they realize it or not. The suggested neutral base colors and their various shades and tones express, among other qualities, taste, tradition, sophistication, serenity, security, dignity, and practicality. All good choices for troubled times.

*And . . . a few final color facts:*

- Colors on the warm end of the color spectrum—red, orange, yellow— are advancing colors that can make you look heavier. Cool hues—blue, purple, and green—are receding colors that can help minimize your size.
- Silver jewelry usually looks best with the cool colors, gold with the warmer tones.
- I use the words *tints, tones, shades,* and *hues* here more or less inter- changeably to simply mean *color,* but for the record there are some technical differences that you should know about in case you ever get on *Jeopardy: Hue* basically does mean *color.* Tints, tones, and shades are variations of pure colors that are formed by adding white, gray, or black, respectively, to one of the major colors of the color wheel. So, for example, add white to pure red and you get pink—a *tint.* Add gray to pure green and you produce sage—a *tone.* And black added to pure purple makes aubergine, or eggplant—a deep *shade* of purple.

As long as you keep one pattern dominant and stay in the same color family you can mix all the prints and patterns you want. But it's a good idea to take it slow at first as your eye develops.

# CHAPTER 4

# Fabrics and Textures

The fourth basic design element of *all* fashion is fabric, and above all else *good fabric makes good clothes.* Fabric, after all, is the backbone of every garment. If the backbone is weak, the whole look falls apart—not to mention the garment itself.

Material, though, provides more than just the actual cloth, it also supplies *texture,* and a clever interplay of textures can be just as fashion effective as the right blend of colors. Textures can add dimension, interest, and surprise to an outfit, as well as broaden the uses of classic shapes—all of which is especially important in a wardrobe primarily based on solids. Jacquards, for example, in which designs are woven right into the fabric, can create sophisticated patterns within a simple monotone outfit, allowing you the benefits of one allover color plus the added interest of a pattern.

Textures can also affect your mood. A pair of black leather trousers, for instance, would not only present quite a different image than the same style trouser in black silk but also would no doubt put you in a more, well, aggressive frame of mind. And, lastly, texture and fabric broadcast messages. Silk charmeuse says rich and sensuous. Corduroy states practical. Lace whispers feminine and delicate. Denim proclaims grit and substance, and double knit polyester mutters pass the bologna sandwich.

The texture of a fabric is determined not just by its fiber content (silk, cotton, linen, wool, etc.) but also by the type of yarn, weave, and fabric finish. So one fiber can make for a huge assortment of textures. Cotton, for instance, produces such diverse fabrics as corduroy, denim, and velour. And silk fiber can be turned into such seemingly unrelated materials as velvet and charmeuse.

Working with textures is actually a lot of fun—mainly because it's so easy. Since there are no rules about what should be worn with what these days you really can't make a mistake as such. (Bad choices maybe—but never a verified mistake.) You can mix totally dissimilar textures such as corduroy with silk or velvet with denim, or create very subtle sophisticated mixes with contrasting pattern knits or different weaves of wool. Today it's a purely personal choice.

The main thing is to be *aware* of textural differences and to gradually incorporate the concept into your everyday dressing. Search through your closet for texture mixes you might not have previously thought of—smooth with rough, shiny with matte, flat knits with bulky ones, or even a dressy metallic with an earthy fabric like denim. And remember that the element of surprise can add character to an outfit. Unexpected contrasts show creativity, imagination, and individuality. *Alert:* Some previously unexpected textural mixes have become so common as to verge on the banal. Lace and leather, for instance, a favorite of the MTV chic crowd, used to be fun because it was slightly shocking. Now it's just tired. So with texture mixes, as with all aspects of fashion, just don't get too trendy. When in doubt, keep it subtle.

Another thing to keep in mind is what various textures do—and don't do—for your body. Bulky knits, for instance, definitely make the body—any body—look heavier, and small women can get lost in them. Sheer silks, on the other hand, don't add bulk but can reveal everything that's under them.

## WHICH FABRICS TO CONSIDER

Fabric *quality* is a major part of your total fashion statement. There's no question that all of us would create a very different impression in a suit made out of fine imported linen than we would in one created from 100 percent domestic polyester.

Only a few years ago the term "good fabrics" referred solely to the time-honored natural fibers: cotton, silk, wool, and linen (and fine suedes and leathers). Without doubt those naturals are still tops. But, in all fairness, there are some man-made fibers these days that make pretty good fabrics too—especially those designed for active sportswear. Some of the best synthetics around, in fact, have been cooked up by sports-oriented companies like

Patagonia for their outdoor clothing lines, and can't be beat in terms of warmth and comfort and practicality.

Since duality of purpose is part of the nineties' fashion creed, a lot of items originally designed for exercise, skiing, sailing, hiking, biking, or camping have infiltrated our everyday wardrobes and become staples of sorts: Lycra and spandex leotards and leggings are practically fashion classics, lightweight nylon parkas make superpackable vacation warmer-uppers, and nobody who lives north of the Mason-Dixon line can deny the value of an indispensable, comfy, down-filled jacket, which is almost always made with a lightweight synthetic shell.

Synthetics have also proven themselves worthy in combination with the naturals. They're generally blended to bring down fabric cost and/or to help counter inherent natural fiber shortcomings. Add just the right dash of polyester and linen can become crease resistant, cotton shrink resistant, and wools and silks machine washable. In general, the higher the percentage of synthetic fiber added, the fewer natural properties that fabric will have, and vice versa. So a 40 percent silk–60 percent polyester blend would theoretically be more geared for wash and wear, but not breathe as well or last as long as pure silk. Man-made textiles, however, are improving rapidly, and this decade is bound to see some awesome advances that could easily change that ratio.

In terms of chic, the bottom line with blends—and even the better synthetics—is this: They are viable choices as long as they look and feel *more natural* than synthetic. Synthetics, after all, were originally designed to simulate their natural counterparts, and for my money they ought to do just that.

The real warning is to steer clear of 100 percent polyester double knits, twills, or gabardines, blatantly acrylic knits, ersatz suede, simulated leather, and flagrantly phony silks. Those kinds of fabrics really have no place in a well-thought-out wardrobe—budget or no budget. Saving money need not be synonymous with second-rate.

Practically speaking, unless you're a forest ranger, an aerobics instructor, or a river guide, your best bet is still to build your everyday wardrobe foundation with natural fabrics and let the man-mades augment and support (sometimes literally). In other words, the *majority* of basic elements in your wardrobe—jackets, slacks, skirts, blouses, dresses. and sweaters—should be made from natural fabrics, or, at the very least, very high-quality blends.

## THE NATURALS

Natural fibers are, of course, derived from natural sources—either plant or animal—and ultimately produce the most varied and sophisticated fabrics and textures in the world. The lushest and most glorious of these, unfortunately, also tend to be the most expensive fabrics in the world. A lot of goats, after all, have to be fed, grazed, and shorn to produce a cozy cashmere cape. And it takes thousands of extremely well-tended little silkworms several weeks to turn out enough silk for just one designer blouse. A lot of skill and labor goes into making quality fabrics, and somebody has to pay for it. Unless you hit the sales just right, that somebody is usually you.

But not to worry. The whole idea of *Dress Like a Million* is fine-tuning and paring down your wardrobe anyway. So while it definitely pays to have some classic, timeless garments made of the highest caliber cloth in your wardrobe, you don't need that many. Our theory is always *quality over quantity*. It's ultimately much wiser to buy a few good things that will serve you elegantly for years, than a slew of mediocre ones that have to be replaced every season. It's wiser for you individually in terms of chic, time, and money, and wiser for all of us in terms of environmental impact.

Although it's not a pleasant thought, I have to at least mention here that even though there are some ecologically conscious companies like Ecosport, Espirit (their Ecollection line), and Higgins Natural that use organically grown cotton, low-impact dyes, and natural buttons (recycled glass and tagua nuts), most clothing made today—whether it's comprised of synthetic or natural fibers—has some sort of negative effect on the environment. Petroleum-based synthetics pollute during the refining processes. Powerful pesticides, fertilizers, and defoliants are often used in growing some natural plant fibers. And harmful chemicals are introduced during the spinning, finishing, and cleaning processes. Even wool-producing sheep, cute as they may be, turn out to be some of the most destructive grazers in the animal kingdom. So don't feel deprived if the economy forces you to buy fewer clothes. Look at it this way: You're actually a hero doing your progeny and your planet a real favor.

### *Cotton*

That said, we still need *some* clothes—and cotton is a good place to start. It is comfortable, affordable, practical, washable, durable, versatile, absorbent, and great looking. In other words it's totally compatible with the nineties.

Cotton fibers can be made into a huge variety of fabrics that run the gamut from the toughest canvas through terry cloth, flannel, and denim to

Cotton can be made into a slew of fabulous fabrics that are perfect for casual wear. This outfit combines denim, corduroy, and fine cotton jersey.

the finest polished Egyptian cotton. The quality of cotton cloth is primarily dependent on the species of cotton from which it's derived. Technically the longest, finest fibers produce the best fabrics, but I won't bore you with the fine science of fabric making here. The bottom line with cotton—and all other fabrics for that matter—is *look and feel,* and the key word is *comparison.*

Whether you're buying a cashmere sweater or a cotton T-shirt you owe it to yourself—and your pocketbook—to check out top-quality merchandise first before shopping for bargain-basement specials. Notice how quality fabrics feel substantial and luxurious, while inferior material feels thin, papery, and stiff. Being able to discern the different qualities of fabric is not a mystery. It's simply a matter of training your visual and tactile senses. It's caring enough to take a few extra minutes whenever you're in a store to stop, focus on, and feel fabrics. Or you could even stop by the best fabric store in your area and compare bolts of pricey fabrics with the cheap ones. Whatever time you spend will be well worth it, since fabric awareness is reflected in both your overall look and your shopping success. When you can recognize good fabrics—with or without a label—you can always be assured you're getting what you're paying for.

> *FYI—some common cotton terms you may run across:*
> - *Egyptian cotton* is smooth, silky, and generally considered the finest in the world—and the most expensive. It's grown in Egypt's fertile Nile valley, but in many cases the raw cotton is shipped to Italy or Asia to be made into fabric, since Egypt never really got its manufacturing act totally together.
> - *Indian cotton* is probably the least expensive. Hippies wore it a lot in the seventies, and preppies have always loved it in its Madras incarnation. It's grown, woven, manufactured, and dyed in small villages in India, usually without the use of chemicals—so we're talking pure, natural fabric here. It's generally a bit coarse with little slubs and nubs spun into the threads, but what it lacks in elegance it makes up for in comfort—it's incredibly cool and light for summer, best for casual and beach wear.
> - *Pima cotton* is American grown—mostly in Arizona and California. It's a hybrid of the native cotton planted by southwestern Indians and Egyptian cotton. A good, strong, silky cotton.
> - *Sea Island cotton* is grown mostly in the West Indies, Florida, Texas, South Carolina, and on the islands off the coast of Georgia. Like pima cotton it's strong and lustrous.
> - *Mercerized cotton* is cotton that's been treated for mildew resistance, extra strength, and a silky, long-lasting luster.

COTTON—QUALITIES AND CARE

Cotton is soft (and gets softer with every washing), practically hypoallergenic, and never sticky or scratchy like wool. It can be either knitted or woven—loosely for summer coolness or tightly for winter warmth—produces no static electricity so won't cling or attract dirt as readily as synthetics, and doesn't pick up body odor like synthetics or fade and get stained by perspiration like silk. What a fabric!

Since cotton fibers actually get stronger when they're wet, cottons can be washed in very hot water. They do, however, mildew easily, so don't leave damp cotton clothes wadded up, and unless they're Sanforized or similarly treated, 100 percent cotton garments will shrink at least 3 percent in washing or dry-cleaning. It's not a great idea to dry-clean cottons since they tend to get dingy in the process.

## Silk

If cotton is the most practical natural fiber, silk is the most luxurious. It's been the treasured fabric of royalty and the aristocracy since that fateful day almost 5,000 years ago when the Chinese empress Si-Ling-Chi accidentally discovered the lustrous fibers of a silkworm cocoon. Today silk still exudes a quiet understated elegance that no other fabric can match.

Because silks are sophisticated and feminine without being fussy, sensual without being overtly sexy, and rich and successful looking without being ostentatious or intimidating, they are an indispensable part of a nineties' wardrobe. How much a part, of course, depends on your life-style. Obviously our hypothetical forest ranger would have less use for silk than a CEO.

But regardless of your occupation, it's a good idea to have at least a few basic silks in your closet for those inevitable and unsettling times when appropriate dress is questionable. *When in doubt silk can often bail you out.* Because the very texture of silk automatically upgrades any look it's hard to look *under*dressed in it. And as long as the design of your outfit is simple and understated it's nearly impossible to look *over*dressed. Add to that the fact that silk easily crosses from day to night, summer to winter, and work to weddings and you've got yourself one superversatile fabric.

Silk comes in a huge assortment of luscious fabrics and textures ranging from the most gossamer chiffons and organzas to the plushest velvets and brocades. But since the nineties is a sensible and practical decade our best bets fall somewhere in between: crepe de chine, charmeuse, quality broadcloth, raw silk, shantung, and Go-silk.

Go-silk, an Eighties' invention, is the most recent addition to silk textures. It's that wonderful, heavy silk you've seen in the stores that feels sort

Even a double-breasted
suit becomes more
feminine, lush, and
drapable when made
from silk.

of velvety and looks dressy with slightly casual overtones. Go-Silk is actually the name of the company that invented the process for "washed silk" and created the term "sandwashed" silk, but the name has become, more or less, the generic term for all washed silk. If you haven't discovered Go-silk yet, you have to check it out. It's a wonderful fabric for almost everything —including jackets.

An ideal silk jacket will have the same qualities you'd like to find in any jacket: impeccable tailoring, great fit, and brilliant design. But when it comes to silk dresses and blouses you also want to look for great drape. Good medium- to heavy-weight silk falls and drapes a lot more gracefully than poor-quality thin silk.

Quality detection is basically on your shoulders. The words "pure silk" on a label simply mean no metallic salts have been added, but do not indicate weight, weave, or quality. So, again, you have to comparison shop. Note that good-quality silk has a nice substantial feel to it, while poor-quality silk usually feels thin and flimsy. About the only time you can get away with thin, cheap silk is in summer shells that are supposed to look gossamer, and in blouses that you *always* wear under jackets or cardigans. The more monochromatic your color scheme, the less noticeable your quality indiscretion. The rest of your outfit will generally carry the look.

*FYI—a very basic silk glossary:*
- *Broadcloth* (aka *China silk*) is the most common and least expensive of the good silks. You can generally find simple silk broadcloth shells and camisoles on sale in department stores for around $20. It's light-weight, smooth, and soft with a subtle luster.
- *Crepe de chine* is woven from a specially twisted yarn that creates a slightly crinkled, lustrous surface. Crepe de chine wrinkles less than broadcloth, but it is more expensive.
- *Charmeuse* is heavier, expensive silk in a smooth, plain weave with a wonderful drape and satiny luster.
- *Chiffon* is a weightless and wonderfully diaphanous silk that works especially well for scarves and layered fantasy gowns.
- *Georgette* is a semitransparent, weightless, wrinkle-resistant crepe that has a slightly grainy feel.
- *Shantung* is a heavy, nubby silk with distinguishing slubs running across the fabric. Great for jackets and suits.
- *Pongee* is a lightly textured, usually cream- to tan-colored silk that's woven with varying width yarns of wild silk. (Wild silk, aka *tussah,* is coarser, less lustrous, and browner.) Again, a natural for summer jackets and suits.

- *Raw silk* is wound directly from several cocoons skipping a few refining processes. It lacks the luster of fine reeled silk, but is less expensive and suitable for jackets.

### SILK—QUALITIES AND CARE

Silk's number one quality, of course, is beauty. No other fabric has the luster of good silk or takes to dye and printing as gloriously. Silk is light-weight, not bulky or confining, provides good insulation, and is durable. Since silk is the strongest of the natural fibers, good silk won't tear or fray as easily as you might think—and it lasts. Although I doubt this will have an impact on your current personal wardrobe, you might find it comforting to know that some 1,200-year-old silk garments, like Charlemagne's silk coronation gown, circa A.D. 800, are still in mint condition.

Many silks have to be dry-cleaned, but some broadcloths, crepe de chines, shantungs, and Go-silks can be hand washed. Check the garment care instruction label. When hand washing is indicated, Go-silk recommends washing in cool water with delicate-washing liquids like Ivory Liquid or Johnson & Johnson baby shampoo. Even Woolite, they say, may be too harsh. Don't rub the garment while washing, since silk fibers weaken when wet. Rinse and machine dry garments on *delicate* cycle at a *cool* or *medium* temperature setting to retain softness, or press dry in a towel. Don't squeeze or ring out. When garments are slightly damp, shake out and hang on padded hangers (not in the sun) to dry completely. If the garment needs ironing, iron when damp. More constructed garments, like jackets, of course, should not be washed by hand.

*Other care tips:*
- Use caution when hand washing dark colors or bright patterns since they tend to run. And don't hand wash chiffon or georgette.
- Apply cold water to a spot immediately if possible—and try to keep it damp to keep the stain from setting until you get it to the cleaners. If you do, experts say even stubborn stains like coffee and red wine can be removed.
- Always check silk clothes before hanging them back in the closet. Spots are much easier to remove when they're new.
- Take silks out of their plastic bags when they come back from the cleaners. Natural fibers need to breathe.
- Excess perspiration will stain silks. Wear guards or a T-shirt under your silk tops if necessary.
- Use silk or cotton thread to hem or alter silks. Polyester thread is too thick for silk and will cause puckering.

## Wool

The way I see it, wool is a miracle fabric. It's incredibly warm, dirt and water resistant, and flame retardant. Since wool fibers are elastic and have a natural tendency to spring back to their original shape, it's also wrinkle and tear resistant and can be altered without leaving telltale old seam- or hemlines. And wool is gorgeous to boot. You just can't beat the look of quality cashmeres, flannels, tweeds, and gabardines. They may not be cheap, but they last forever.

You can create wonderful, sophisticated outfits simply by mixing and matching wool textures.

Wool quality is largely dependent on the breed and care of the sheep and the complexities of the various manufacturing processes. Labels rarely hint of either. With the exception, perhaps, of the Woolmark label, which is used by more than ten thousand manufacturers internationally and does indicate good quality, labels here are merely a guarantee of content—not quality. The term "virgin wool," for instance, signifies wool that hasn't been manufactured into fabric before—as opposed to "reprocessed wool," which has been made from scraps and mill ends. A label reading "merino wool" lets you know that the original fiber comes from merino sheep. When it comes right down to it, when assessing wool quality, you really, once again, have to fall back on your sense perceptions. Quality wool has a softness, a fine, close, even weave, a springy warm feel, and a pleasingly substantial weight. Inferior wools tend to be stiff, scratchy, and a tad dull.

*FYI—a few very basic terms:*
- *Tweed* is a fabric with tiny colored slubs of yarn woven in. The more supple, the better the tweed. The two most famous are probably *Donegal* tweed, which is woven by hand in County Donegal, Ireland, and *Harris* tweed, which is woven from vegetable dyed yarns on the island of Harris and Lewis off the west coast of Scotland. It's thick, soft, and usually expensive.
- *Herringbone* is a subtle twill weave with a tiny V pattern.
- *Houndstooth* check has a pattern of broken checks woven into the fabric.
- *Gabardine* is a light twill fabric that can be woven so finely that it drapes and falls like heavy silk. It can theoretically also be woven from cotton, rayon, or synthetics. If you could own only one pair of slacks I'd recommend they be made of top-quality wool gabardine.
- *Worsted wool* is a lightweight, smooth, finely woven wool with a nice drape. It's comfortable in all seasons except the steamiest months of summer. Another good choice for slacks and suits.

## WOOL CARE

Wool doesn't like direct heat, so wrinkles should be pressed out with steam—never a dry iron. Most skirts, jackets, and slacks have to be dry-cleaned.

Knitted wools can be hand washed gently (knead, don't rub, since hard rubbing frays the fibers) in Woolite or Ivory Snow in lukewarm water. Never use hot water unless you're purposely trying to shrink a garment. Always rinse thoroughly. Some experts advise a quick dousing in diluted vinegar before the final rinse to remove any soap remnants and perk up colors. Dry flat.

Wash or dry-clean wool garments at the end of the season, then store in sealed garment bags or a cedar-lined chest, which will help repel hungry moths. Stay away from moth-proofing compounds, since they can be as hazardous to *your* health as the moths'.

While we're on the subject of health hazards, dry-cleaning is not that good for you either. Most dry cleaners use a solvent called perchloroethylene that fouls the air, causes cancer in animals, and has been classified by the U.S. Environmental Protection Agency as a *probable human carcinogen. Consumer Reports* says we're likely to be exposed to some level of perc just by wearing recently dry-cleaned clothes or storing them in the house. They suggest the following:

- Dry-clean clothes only to clean them—not to remove wrinkles or bagginess, these can be taken care of with a quick pressing.
- Hang freshly dry-cleaned clothes in the open air—preferably by a window for a day or two—before storing them.
- Don't store newly dry-cleaned clothes in the kid's room, since children are more sensitive to toxins than adults.
- If your clothes come back from your dry cleaner reeking of chemicals take your business elsewhere.

## Linen

Linen is a supercool summer fabric, since it absorbs moisture and dries faster than almost any other fabric. It's also soil resistant, washable, sophisticated, and incredibly durable. In fact, it runs neck and neck with cotton for the oldest-textile-known-to-man title. Fragments of linen were discovered in Stone Age dwellings, Egyptian mummies were wrapped in it, and the shroud of Turin is made of it. All to say, it's another one of those fabrics that, bar any miraculous genetic discoveries, will probably last longer than you will.

Linen's main drawbacks today are its cost and lack of versatility. Since producing linen is an especially tricky, esoteric art that requires tremendous dedication and skill—not to mention perfectly pure water, which is why most of the best linen still comes from Ireland and Belgium—it can be quite expensive. Combine that with the fact that linen is essentially a one-season fabric that doesn't travel or drape particularly well, and I'm afraid that as much as I personally love it, it falls somewhat short of being indispensable. But even so, should you happen upon a *particularly good deal* on a fabulous basic linen shirt, jacket, or other wardrobe staple, you really can't go wrong buying it—especially if you live in a tropical or semitropical climate. Colorwise, whites and naturals are surer bets since linen doesn't dye well.

Linen is terrifically cool in hot weather, but since it doesn't drape particularly well it's best suited for straighter, slightly tailored lines.

Linen does wrinkle. To wear it well you simply have to accept that fact and wear the creases proudly. If you've got a problem with that, forget about linen. You could go the wrinkle-resistant-linen route, but according to some experts when linen is treated for wrinkle resistance it doesn't breathe as well as the pure variety, it scorches easily, and looses some of its strength. I personally don't think it looks as good either.

*FYI—A few bonus terms:*

- *Moygashel* is the name of an Irish company that produces high-quality Irish linen, used to make clothing.
- *Handkerchief linen* (or *cambric*) is by all accounts the softest linen available. The best comes from Ireland where they've been spinning linen for 1,500 years and definitely have it down to a fine science.
- *Oatmeal linen* is an unbleached oatmeal-colored homespun-type fabric used for blazers. It's usually imported from Poland and is generally cheaper than handkerchief linen.
- *Oyster linen* is unbleached off-white homespun-type linen. Again less expensive than handkerchief.

## LINEN CARE

Linen can be hand washed in Woolite and lukewarm water—although, again, this is not recommended for structured jackets and the like. No vinegar rinses for linen as vinegar burns the fabric. Iron linen when wet. Most linen irons so beautifully that some people find pressing it thoroughly therapeutic—a bonus.

## Rayon

I'm including rayon here with the natural fibers because, while it's not a *true* natural, it is rebuilt from natural wood pulp, which leaves it teetering on the fence between natural and synthetic. Rayon, the royal patriarch of man-made fibers, was originally designed back in the 1880s to look like silk. These days you can find it disguised as cotton, wool, and linen as well.

Rayon, also called viscose, is actually a good, viable fabric for today's wardrobe. It breathes fairly well, is delightfully cool, has a nice drape, and since some top designers use it, there are good-looking rayon garments on the market—and they're usually reasonably priced.

Rayon, however, is not as strong as the natural fibers, so it's not great for heavy knocking about. Again, with rayon as with other fabrics, there are poor and good qualities of cloth. Some rayons lack elasticity and can bag, separate at the seams, and wrinkle easily. If you tug gently at the seams of a rayon garment and it looks like the seams could open, think about reinforcing them *before* you wear the garment.

Rayon, a semisynthetic with a natural feel, is making a comeback with some of the better designers. Soft and fluid, rayon's a natural for light summer dresses and skirts.

## LEATHERS

Sumptuous, supple suedes and leathers can be incredibly good-looking—and, unfortunately, incredibly expensive. My suggestion: If you can't afford truly top-quality leather, forgo the experience altogether. There's no doubt that a fabulous leather jacket is a great investment. It can be worn over almost anything, always looks chic, is a great windbreaker, can add pizzazz to ordinary outfits, elevates your entire look immediately, and improves with wear and age. There's also no doubt that a low-grade leather jacket is hard and stiff and tacky. Cheap leather looks cheap and is unacceptable. Period.

If you do decide to splurge on leather, don't forget to check the sales. Most stores reduce leather items right along with coats and other winter merchandise when they need to make room for the new spring lines. But remember that maintenance can be high—as much as $35 to clean a simple pair of suede slacks. So consider darker shades that show dirt less and can be cleaned more easily.

These days wearing leather, like wearing fur, can also be somewhat political. Animal rights organizations discourage it. Since most leathers are food industry by-products, it's certainly easier to justify wearing leather than fur, which comes from animals that are slaughtered expressly for their pelts. Neither, of course, is a necessity in this day and age. In the long run it's a matter of individual conscience. I personally still feel OK about wearing leather from domesticated sources (maybe as I get more enlightened I'll change my mind), but I meticulously avoid anything made from wild or endangered species like alligator, lizard, peccary, snakes, etc. As for fur, I just can't do it anymore. I simply don't want animals killed on my account.

## BEADED CLOTHING

And last but not least, a word about *beaded clothes.* Beading, just in case you're as confused as I once was, doesn't just mean *beads.* The term also encompasses *sequins,* those small sparkling plastic discs with a thread hole in the center; *paillettes,* overlarge sequins that are also called spangles, and *rhinestones,* which are diamondlike stones made from cut glass. Bugle beads, tiny multicolored cylindrical pieces of glass or plastic, are still the most popular style of beading. You'll see bugle beads a lot in Hollywood on Oscar night and every night at the circus. Most beaded antique jackets and sweaters are made with bugle beads.

A simple dark beaded dress or top would be a very handy thing to have in your wardrobe, since you could just pop it on for every gala affair. The trick is finding one that's exquisitely cut at a reasonable price. Inexpensive machine-made beaded garments usually don't hang well and tend to fall apart when you look at them sideways. And the crème de la crème of beaded clothing can be very expensive; indeed in the thousands of dollars for a designer garment. But if you're a good thrift-store shopper you can still find wonderful beaded wool sweaters from the fifties for under $50, lovely beaded rayon jackets from the thirties for between $100 and $150, and if you're really lucky, a dress for $200 or so. Almost-new shops are another good possible source. (See Chapter 7.) Always do a thorough check to see that the beads are sewn on well and there are none missing.

Beaded garments can be tricky to maintain. Cheap sequins have been known to melt in dry-cleaning solutions. It's best to buy dark colors that can go the distance with minimal or no cleaning. All glass beads are hand washable and dry-cleanable but are difficult to iron, so it's best to have glass-beaded garments spot cleaned or dry-cleaned—infrequently.

A final reminder: With the possible exception of beaded material, the bottom line with fabrics is *feel*. Good fabrics will always feel better than poor-quality fabrics. If there's any doubt in your mind as to the quality of a fabric do a comparison test. The final test is always in the touch.

# CHAPTER 5

# Million-Dollar Strategies . . .

## THE ESSENCE OF NINETIES' DRESSING

Now that you've got a good working knowledge of the main fashion principles, you're ready for the basic *Dress Like a Million* strategies. These are the major concepts that will help you slide stylishly through this decade on less cash—and with less stress. Many of these ideas, as promised, are integral components of the general directional trends we discussed in Chapter 1. We'll just be taking the liberty of lending new interpretations and making slight variations on a theme, when called for.

## UNIFORM DRESSING

Uniform dressing, for instance, is very big with the MTV chic pack. In its purest form it's a wonderfully viable concept, since it puts fashion on automatic pilot and frees the mind to explore bigger and better things. The problem with the terminally trendy MTV-chic approach to uniforms is (1) they don't know they're doing it and (2) they all wear the same uniform. Bad idea. *Uniform dressing only works when you come up with your own perfect uniform—not someone else's.* Obviously that also rules out nurses' whites and policemen's blues.

Uniform dressing for our purposes essentially means two things. (1) Building your wardrobe around a *limited* set of styles, lines, and colors that are perfectly suited to your body, personality, and life-style *and sticking to them* so that your general silhouette, in effect, becomes your uniform. And (2) putting together a few actual outfits within that context that are perfect for various occasions and that you can pull out of your closet, put on, and look fabulous in, almost without thinking.

Writer Tom Wolfe is a world-class champion uniform dresser, and should serve as an inspiration to us all. He's been wearing double-breasted white suits so long he's become practically synonymous with them. He's totally fashionable without being fashiony, and always looks dapper and totally himself. I bet when *he* gets a last-minute request for an impromptu meeting

Marlene Dietrich and Katharine Hepburn dressed in men's trousers and jackets for decades. Now it's finally caught on. It's one way—but not the only way—to approach uniform dressing.

he never cries "Oh my god, what am I going to wear?" Actually, men have teetered on the edge of uniform dressing since Adam donned his first fig leaf. Today the foliage has simply been replaced by a suit for business; jeans, chinos, or sweats for leisure; and a tux for very formal occasions.

I'm not suggesting, of course, that we dress like men, although that is a legitimate option, and one, I might add, that didn't seem to have any adverse effect on Katharine Hepburn or the late Marlene Dietrich. I'm simply suggesting ultimate paring down, not just in the actual amount of clothes in your wardrobe, but in the variety of styles too. Not only will you need fewer accessories (a limited selection of shoe and bag styles, for instance, will tend to go with a lot more outfits), but it will actually help you establish a real personal style. Here's how one very fashionable friend of mine, a svelte-looking size 14, who has been referred to as "the best camouflage dresser since Stormin' Norman," describes *her* uniform:

> I generally wear all one color skirt and top. Most always a black skirt with a black camisole or some kind of black tank top. I have that variation in linen, Go-silk, and rayon. I belt it with a black belt, usually trimmed in gold or something else fun. Then I wear a jacket or some other kind of top over it; a short top if it's a long skirt, and a long top if it's a short skirt. My jackets usually have a small print or a small check. Sometimes I'll go with a wild print, but always with black in it. I usually go for black and turquoise, black and red, black and fuchsia . . . always a black background. My clothes are never bulky. They're always a very smooth material—silk is great—and usually unstructured and unlined. I like things with lapels but I sometimes wear shawl collars.
>
> When I wear my small-printed jackets I try to wear a scarf—a long oblong scarf knotted low—in some color that picks up whatever is going on. If the jacket has a *very* small print, I'll wear a complementary print scarf. With my red-and-black herringbone tweed, for instance, I wear a red-and-black very small polka-dotted scarf. I have about a half dozen pairs of black shoes. And that's basically what I find myself wearing. It's a very specific look. Now when I look in my closet I have all the same kinds of things. But that's OK by me. My motto is "If it has black in it it's gotta be good."

Your uniform, of course, can take any form depending on your personal likes, your body shape, and your life-style. Lean-line pants, a simple shirt, cardigan, and ballet-slipper flats, for instance, is a silhouette that could work well for a slim Audrey Hepburn type who worked in the arts. Short skirts, T-shirts, and unstructured jackets could form a winning uniform foundation for a TV producer (with good legs). Long skirts, large, belted overblouses, and jackets might be a great everyday look for a full-figured saleswoman. You get the idea; the actual pieces can change, but the general shapes and lines stay somewhat constant. Other possibilities: loose slacks and tunics; jeans and a tweed or navy blazer with white shirt and cowboy boots; khakis, white shirt, and Topsiders; turtleneck, tucked overblouse, and trousers; T-shirt and jodphurs; slouchy pantsuits, etc., etc.

Life-style, of course, is key here. A woman who works in a corporate environment is obviously going to need totally different everyday uniforms than a woman who works at home or in a casual, laid-back situation. Most of us will need a few uniforms—one for work, one for play, one for dressy evenings, and, if you're a big event goer, a fourth, maybe something beaded, would be handy.

Recently most of my days have been spent in my home office writing this book. Not surprisingly, a "work uniform" evolved of its own volition: black leggings, a roomy white mock turtleneck, and some sort of big over sweater in one of my colors (black, white, red, turquoise, or blue), white socks, and sneakers. If it's exceptionally cold I put on some black leg warmers and a thermal undershirt. It's a perfect uniform for this chapter of my life (and this chapter of the book.) It's comfortable. The individual components are inexpensive and readily available (so I always have a fresh set ready to go). It's presentable enough to do errands in or even step out for a quick meeting or casual dinner when topped with a long leather jacket and great scarf. But the real bonus is that I don't have to think about what I'm going to wear every day. I just get up and get dressed. And that, of course, is the whole idea behind uniform dressing.

Uniform dressing doesn't mean you can never wear anything else. Obviously my uniform will change come summer, and I could get tired of leggings tomorrow. *Uniforms are not carved in stone.* They last for an undefined period of time—ranging from a few weeks to forever—and are usually related to what's going on in your life. Once they've run their course, you move on to your next uniform—hopefully incorporating some pieces and shapes from the old one. Uniforms take on new dimensions and evolve naturally as fashion shifts and we change.

In an office, you'll probably want a bit more variety than I need when I work at home, but you should still try to stick as closely as possible to the same *general motif.* You don't have to wear something *entirely* different every day. That's truly archaic thinking. If you're a pants person, or love long skirts or vests, wear them a lot and let them become part of your personal style. You don't *have to* wear them every day—we all need a change occasionally. But it's very comforting to always have a look to fall back on that never fails and that is quintessentially you. The stricter the dress codes are in your profession, the more you'll come to appreciate the uniform-dressing concept.

The truth is that most people won't even consciously realize that you're wearing more or less the same designs. They'll just subconsciously think of them as your style. They're more apt to be aware of a consistent color palette, but that's to be admired these days. Today it's even perfectly acceptable to wear the same jacket, skirt, or sweater a few days a week. This is the conscious nineties (well, semiconscious anyway), after all, not the consumer-driven eighties.

Oh, and don't be embarrassed to buy multiples. A friend of mind recently confessed, somewhat sheepishly, that when she finds something she absolutely loves—a perfect skirt, pair of pants, jacket, blouse, sweater, or whatever—she buys a few of them, sometimes even in the same color! She likes to have a reserve. It's a great idea if you can afford it. The warning here is often that what works well in one color might not be all that smashing in another. I recently found a great sweater in black and went back to buy another just like it in turquoise. Somehow it didn't look as special in turquoise, and I ended up returning it. So take heed.

## JACKET DRESSING

Jackets are the number one wardrobe staple of the nineties, mainly because they're extremely practical, versatile, and easy to wear. They can be paired with almost anything from jeans to dresses to leggings. They dress up very casual outfits, always add a dash of style, are cross seasonal, and provide an extra layer of (easily removable) warmth as well as very usable pockets. Plus they are relatively trend proof.

So the question here isn't really whether jackets should be an integral part of your wardrobe, but rather how many and what style. The answer to both these questions primarily depends on your budget. Simply put, the less money you have to spend, the less you can afford to splurge on styles of questionable longevity. Classics (in black or one of our nontrendy neutrals) are incredibly versatile and will remain fashionable a lot longer than their voguish counterparts, meaning you'll get a lot more wear out of them across the board. Once you have one or two perfect classics you can supplement them with alternative styles if you like.

The most classic jacket around is the blazer, basically a loose-fitting tailored jacket that was first worn by Cambridge University cricket players

Jackets are indispensable nineties' wardrobe staples. Get a nontrendy classic style first, then supplement with variations on the theme when your budget allows.

in the late nineteenth century (more fabulous fashion trivia). Today, blazers come in all sorts of fabrics, and their shapes vary. There are double-breasted and single-breasted varieties; some are more fitted than others; lengths and lapel widths differ; and then there's detailing like pockets, trimming, and buttons.

So how to choose the perfect all-around blazer for you? It's back to basics. Think fabric first. It should be top grade. A blazer is one of those investment items that should provide a *minimum* of five years of stylish wear. In a four-season climate it would be ideal to have a fine wool and cashmere and/or tweed blazer for fall, winter, and the cool days of spring and a nubby silk, Go-silk, linen, or light wool gabardine blazer for summer and warm spring and fall days.

Next think of your body type and proportions. In general, full-bodied women (Rose types) do better with the single-breasted blazers. Thin women can wear single- or double-breasted blazers. If you're narrow on top and full on the bottom (Tulip or Orchid) look for roomy, full blazers that will help balance the proportional discrepancy. Classic blazer length is just below the buttocks, but do an individual assessment here. If you have short legs and wear mostly skirts, for instance, you might want to hem your blazer a tad shorter to make your legs look longer. If you have heavy thighs but love the comfort of leggings, a longer jacket could help the balance.

Color? Your base neutrals or very complementary tones for your first summer and winter blazers. Any of your accent tones next.

Regardless of what style jacket you opt for don't forget to make allowances for what you wear under it. If you wear a lot of big sweaters, buy the next larger size and get the sleeves taken up if necessary.

Also consider your uniform or overall general style. Obviously if you wear a lot of long big tops, a bolero jacket would be an extremely poor style choice for your main jacket. Shawl collars, V necks, and other open-front jackets readily reveal what's underneath, which means you actually have to think "outfit" when you wear them—as opposed to just throwing on something over your sweatshirt. Not a good idea for a first jacket.

As for the top-of-hipbone styles, they simply won't have the staying power of a blazer-type jacket. So they're nice as a novelty, but not as a primary investment (unless they are part of your uniform silhouette and the shape will go with almost everything in your wardrobe). Ditto for boleros. And *stay away from excess detailing*. Simplicity is the key to chic and always will be. Detailing dates a garment as surely as the date stamp on the milk carton. Decorative buttons on unusable flap breast pockets—out. Faux-gold buttons on wannabe safari jackets—forget it. White piping on a classic black jacket —afraid not. Biker jackets—should be déclassé two weeks after you read this book.

One last word on jackets: Don't overlook the viability of men's jackets. Some women find them a godsend. Men's jackets are roomy, well made, and have those great inside breast pockets. Aside from obvious sources, you can often find great deals at secondhand and antique shops, and since jackets are worn over other garments you won't quite feel the presence of the original owner as much you might in a more intimate garment.

Fashion maven Tracey Ross likes men's clothing so much she often buys it to sell to women in her Beverly Hills boutique. "That was my whole thing for the first six months I was open," she says. "I would buy men's vintage jackets. I did really well with them. I think [women's] designers have finally realized they should cut their jackets bigger. Now we're seeing a men's double-breasted tailored suit look, with the trousers a little more pleated and baggy. . . ."

When designers start doing men's tailoring for women you can bet the price goes up. So check the men's stores first. Even better, check the closets of your male friends and relatives. They can be even better sources than secondhand shops. And don't forget—if jackets don't fit perfectly they can be altered. The cost will still be considerably less than that of a new jacket.

Margo Werts, the chic owner of L.A.'s American Rag boutique, which carries wonderful new and used clothes, also wears men's jackets, as well as men's trousers and polo shirts. She points out that today's look in men's clothes for women is more fitted than, say, the Annie Hall look of the seventies. She makes a good point. A stylish nineties' silhouette can still be loose and roomy, but it is neat and manageable, as opposed to oversized and messy.

## BLACK FOREVER

Another winning ploy embraced by the MTV set is black. Ah, if they would only expand their textural horizons beyond spandex and lace.

Black has always been basic and always will be basic. It's such a handy color (or noncolor, if you will) that if you can wear it well you owe it to yourself to seriously consider it as one of your base neutral colors. (See Chapter 3.) Aside from the fact that black is a classic that will never be out of vogue and is always considered chic, black also:

- can be worn night or day
- goes great with everything—even jeans
- conceals dirt, thus requires less maintenance
- travels well
- hides minor detailing flaws
- can be worn more frequently because it's less conspicuous than other colors
- is a wonderful backdrop for interesting jewelry
- looks expensive

And perhaps even more important, black is *always* available in the stores —a big consideration. If you start building a wardrobe on some esoteric, albeit lovely, color you will constantly be in search mode. On the other hand, need today's black skirt to go with yesterday's black jacket? No problem. Plus, there's always that ultimate bonus—black is slimming.

The only instances I've found black to be less than ideal is at weddings, on sunny Caribbean vacations where it feels a tad gloomy, in Greece where it is de rigueur for all widows and old crones, and around white cats. Light-colored poodles, on the other hand, are just terrific around black, since they don't shed hair like regular dogs. (They're also—I have to mention this— quite brilliant and very sweet.)

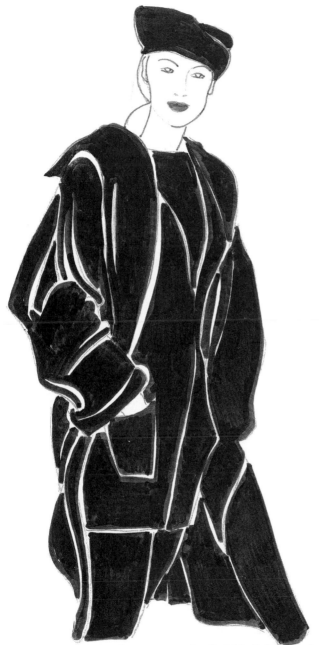

Black is a fashion perennial nonpareil. Mixing and layering various black pieces often makes up a sum that's much greater—and more gorgeous—than its parts.

There are some women, I suppose, who find black boring, but they are usually very rich women who have closets the size of small apartments and who find the concepts of uniformity, speed, and economy rather dull. They are also women who already own every imaginable style there is—probably in black.

## ECLECTICISM AND SURPRISE

The bas couture folks have hit on the right idea when it comes to ferreting out and mixing eclectic pieces. Some of them may tend to overdo it now and then, but the idea is solid. Breaking out of the mold to mix and match unexpected styles or topping off a classic ensemble with a subtle touch of whimsy is a real sign of personal style. It's also one of the things that keeps the classics from getting boring.

For the most part that's exactly what the haute couture designers have been up to lately—new associations of old elements. Let's face it, just about everything has already been done, so there's not much left for them to do but take things out of their traditional context and mix the old with the new, the high with the low. So what do we see on the pages of *Vogue* and *Bazaar?* Business-type suits with lace bustiers, tulle dresses covered with tailored cotton shirts, and leather and denim mixed with satin, organza, and rhinestones. Versace has referred to it as "chic and shock." Basically anyone can do it. In its extreme form it really takes more guts than artistic genius.

I would suggest, however, keeping *your* surprises toned down. A rhinestone choker and leather jacket can look terrific in a picture and maybe even on a runway, but not necessarily in a boardroom. A small rhinestone pin on a tweed jacket, on the other hand, could be smashing. So when you thumb through the pages of fashion magazines look for ideas, then tone them down to real-life dimensions.

You can also add surprise with unusual blends of colors and, as we just discussed, textures or by simply stepping out of your standard look. If, for instance, you're a classically chic dresser, even sneakers would constitute a surprise.

The only other warning here is that this idea of renegade mixing has spawned some styles that have become so mainstream that they're already a cliché. Cowboy boots with diaphanous antique dresses, for instance, was an interesting blend of the romantic with the down-to-earth until it became commonplace. And so was leather and lace before it became la mode de la semaine at rock clubs. So try to think of the surprises yourself. Think about mixing antique with high tech, or something couture with something street, but do it in a way that reflects *your* taste, interests, and likes—a way that is uniquely you.

## RECYCLING

Recycling, of course, is one of the main buzzwords of the nineties, and it should absolutely be applied to fashion. Bas followers are recycling when they shop thrift shops, secondhand stores, and garage sales—all incidentally, excellent places to find bargains if you have the time, patience, and fortitude. (See Chapter 8.)

But you can also recycle straight from your own closet. Chances are there are at least a couple of buried treasures in there that you haven't thought about in years that can be altered, updated, re-accessorized, and generally modernized.

Quality is the bottom line when it comes to recycling. If the fabric and overall design are choice—and the color is flattering to you—it's a good candidate for wardrobe recycling. If it's made from cheap material and/or the color makes you look green, don't waste the gas taking it the tailor. Rather put recycle plan number two into effect and donate it to the homeless; or if it is truly and pathetically nonredeemable consider recycle plan number three—ripping it to shreds and using it for cleaning rags.

Some items worthy of recycling: Jackets pop to mind first since they're such integral wardrobe pieces and quality new ones can be costly. Jacket lapels can be easily reshaped, shoulders can be reset, shoulder pads can be added or subtracted, linings replaced, and hem and sleeve lengths adjusted. Men's jackets are prime recycling candidates, since their cuts are almost always classic, and men's clothes in general tend to be well made. Sandy Duncan had one of her husband's three-piece suits scaled down to her size, and she looks super in it. And my good friend Barbara manages to look chic as always when she wears shoulder pads under her husband's T-shirts. So remember to alert the men in your life that you'd like rights of first refusal on any rejects.

Coats offer recycling potential too. I've seen simple wool reefers turned into a vision of elegance by the simple addition of a fur collar and cuffs. This might be one way to at least get *some* use out of an old fur stole or coat that's too politically incorrect to wear it its present state. I wholeheartedly agree with animal activists in their quest to stop fur trade, but if you've got some thirty-year-old fur lying around that could be made into a shawl collar or used to line a wool coat or denim jacket or even a raincoat . . . well, I can't see that burning it would have any positive effect on the environment.

Obviously extensive alterations require either sewing expertise or an excellent tailor; neither are particularly easy to come by. Finding a good tailor with reasonable prices is like finding a good hairdresser or doctor—you have to ask around, and praying can't hurt. Sometimes it's a matter of trial and

Clip off old silk pajama pants at the knee for a new summer look.

Update oldies but
goodies by wearing them
differently. Here a friendly
old V-necked cardigan
gets a new life by the
simple addition of a belt.

error. But when you do find her (or him), treat her right; she's worth her weight in gold.

One important thing to remember about recycling is that *nothing is too sacred to alter*. It's easy to get cold feet about remodeling an expensive piece of clothing—especially if it has a famous designer label sewn in the back. But don't be intimidated and don't justify procrastination with thoughts like "maybe these wide lapels will come back," or "this skirt is really not *that* bad this length." By the time the wide lapels become stylish again the moths could have had your jacket for dinner. Live in the present. Take it out, get it fixed, and wear it—now. What have you got to lose? You're not wearing it anyway. Clothes are made to be worn, not idolized.

Aside from actual alterations, you can also add new life to older jackets by wearing them differently. Toss a contrasting scarf over it, flip up the lapels, push up the sleeves, add pins and brooches or pair it with a T-shirt and jeans, a long skirt, or even a floaty floral rayon dress if that's your thing.

Look at shirts with an eye for wearing them over or under other shirts or sweaters. Think about removing collars. Sweaters can be tucked in or belted for a new look. Skirts can be restyled by shortening or even adding stretch cotton panels to the top, and then belting big tops over them.

Pants silhouettes, like everything else these days, run the style gamut. They can be narrow, wide, and in between—good news for recyclers. Although it's tough to make slacks wider, it's a piece of cake to taper them. Or in the case of old baggy khakis, simply cut them off, cuff them, and make yourself a nice pair of baggy shorts.

If a garment itself is over-the-hill but the material it's made from is still beautiful, think of other ways you can recycle the fabric. When the sleeve of my favorite kimono-style robe, for instance, was chewed up by an airport conveyor belt (the robe was inside a suitcase that suffered the same ugly fate), first I cried, then had the hole patched with a lovely piece of fine cotton from an old Cacharel blouse. It didn't match perfectly, of course, but it definitely personalized the robe and added character—and history. In fact, in truth I actually liked the robe's look better après accident. I also used to use old fabric to make covers for my steno pads—which actually did seem like a good idea at the time. . . . The only limit to recycling is your imagination.

Also remember that in the long run recycling even fashion—is better for the environment. The planet is in trouble, and if we can do anything, however small, to help out we should. More recycling and *less* consumerism will help.

## LAYERING

In their enthusiasm to combine eclectic looks of yesteryear into a modern potpourri, some bas couture devotees have taken layering to new levels of artistry—another great idea. Layering is the best fashion concept to come out of the seventies and eighties, and it's just as viable in the nineties. We should take advantage of it whenever we can.

Layering, of course, is great for weather variations, but it also allows multiple uses for various garments, which in the long run reduces the amount of clothes we really need.

The main thing to think about when layering in the nineties is, again, silhouette. It's a bit tidier, simpler and cleaner than in previous decades. Layering garments of similar colors and values helps keep the look neat. The nineties is more about wearing a few cardigans at a time, perhaps tied around your neck or waist, than being engulfed in layers of overlarge garments. And vests are still terrific layering components.

## NONSTATUS STATUS SYMBOLS

Another bas concept. In their quiet, often inelegant way the bas folk seem to be telling us that flashy status symbols are no longer necessary. Absolutely true. Designer status symbols are passé. If Gucci and Pucci were the sixties and Halston was the seventies and Ralph Lauren was the eighties, then the Gap is the nineties. And labels, for the most part, are once more where they belong—on the *inside* of our garments.

With the exception perhaps of a Lexus or maybe an electric car, the new status symbols are affordable and egalitarian: Save-the-Whale sweatshirts, ecologically correct decals, and disinterest in material things. Even top designers recognize this fact and are offering less expensive spin-off lines, among them Anne Klein, Ralph Lauren, Ellen Tracy, Ungaro, Armani, Escada, and Perry Ellis. True, you still may get better service in Tiffany's by flashing an old-time status symbol like a gold Rolex, but you might also draw the attention of petty thieves. If one can judge by the spate of Rolex robberies in southern California, yesterday's status symbols are not only semioffensive today, they can be hazardous to your health as well.

## CLASSICS—THE BUILDING BLOCKS OF GREAT WARDROBES

The classic chic crowd gets kudos for this one. Even if you had all the money in the world, you'd want to have some classics in your wardrobe that have the potential of becoming old treasured friends. Classics are those omnipresent thematic fashion perennials that transcend the whims of style and time. They are wardrobe staples that may metamorphose slightly from decade to decade, but will probably be around at least as long as you are.

Although classics seldom seem to make rousing fashion statements on their own, they are dependable garments or accessories that can be counted on year after year—and because they're eminently flexible they always seem

Some time-honored
fashion classics.

to blend flawlessly with the individual style of the wearer. If you can picture Audrey Hepburn in it—it's probably a classic.

The telltales signs of a classic: simplicity of design, top quality and/or extremely practical fabric or materials, durability, versatility, and neutral colors.

Some time-honored classics: the French beret, loafers, sneakers, ballet-slipper flats, espadrilles, the Chanel slingback, a string of pearls, the blazer, the turtleneck, the V-necked pullover, the chemise, straight-legged pleated tailored slacks, the trenchcoat, the cardigan, the silk shirt, the cape.

Every once in a blue moon another style will join the ranks of classics. Jeans, chinos, white cotton shirts, and T-shirts certainly have, and leggings are probably the latest, although in all fairness, they have been around since Elizabethan days. Like I said, the classics have staying power. At this point even the humble sweatshirt can be considered a casual classic.

Recently the glories of "the crisp white shirt" have been expounded upon ad infinitum in the fashion magazines. Although it's being hyped like a fad, I personally feel it meets all the standards of a classic—so I've added it to my list. On the other hand, the white cotton shirt that's tied at the midriff, à la Marilyn in the fifties, is definitely *not* on my list. It's an honesty-of-purpose thing, really. If you were out working in the fields in your white shirt and got hot, you might tie the shirt up, let a little air in. I'd buy that. It's practical, smart. But to buy a shirt that is already tied up for you whether it's hot or not, a shirt that *instructs* you how to wear it . . . I don't think so. It's not honest and it's not smart. It's a fad, pure and simple. Classics are clothes and accessories that *let you mold them,* not vice versa.

## BLUE-CHIP BUYS

Just like your fantasy stock portfolio, every wardrobe needs to include a few choice blue-chip items that will continue to pay good steady dividends over the years. Blue-chip garments and accessories are prime pieces that are 100 percent flattering, totally reflect your essence, and make you feel special every time you wear them. The best blue chips are also wholly in step with your life-style and can be worn for decades. They are, in other words, *individual classics.*

Most of us already own a blue chip or two; that great belt that you seem to wear with everything, that cherished gold pin your grandmother gave you, that beloved black blazer that you toss on without thinking. Obviously, since blue chips are individual by definition, their exact form will be different for all of us, but a few aspects of an ideal classic blue chip are universal:

- The quality of the item should be superb.
- The design should be classic within the context of your personal style.
- It should be versatile enough to be worn often and with many different outfits.
- It should be ultimately complementary and wonderfully comfortable.

If a garment or accessory meets at least four of these standards you've probably got yourself a solid blue chip. Until your trust fund has come through, of course, not every item in your closet can be a blue chip. The idea is to pick one up every now and then when you can afford it—a great jacket here, a wonderful scarf there, a perfect pair of silver earrings, a classic pair of black slacks, etc.—and gradually form a small collection of gems that will lend class and individuality to your wardrobe for years to come.

The important thing to remember in these lean years is that any time you invest an appreciable amount of money on an item, say over $125, it should be a piece with a future. The more money spent, the longer the prospective future.

In the final analysis the real test of an investment buy comes not so much in the original cash outlay, but in the *amortization factor:* how many times did you wear something over how long a period of time. The *true cost* of an item can be tallied by dividing the purchase price by the number of times you wear the article in question. Example: Your favorite jacket cost $300. It's so fabulous and looks so great on you, you wear it three days a week. That's 121 days a year. Divide $300 by 121 days and you get approximately $2.50 per wearing . . . for the first year. The second year your cost per wear would be about $1.24, and by the third year it would be approximately eighty-two cents, and so on. By the time you factor in bonus points for the pure pleasures of wearing it, and the self-confidence and chic it provides, you're well into positive return. Your jacket was a terrific bargain.

Still, it *always* pays to comparison shop—especially when there is a considerable outlay of money. Shop the sales. With retailing in trouble this is a buyer's market. If something strikes your fancy ask the saleswoman to hold it for you while you scout around for a better deal. Most will be more than happy to comply. It's always a good idea to get your salesperson's name and phone number and to call at the end of the day to let her know your intentions—even if you've decided to pass. Good karma is very nineties.

*Warning:* Impulse shopping can be hazardous to your pocketbook. (See Chapter 8.)

## QUALITY

Quality, of course, is a condition of excellence, and in fashion terms that means superlative design, fabric, and workmanship. It also signifies the amount of effort and craftsmanship that goes into an item, and the amount of attention paid to small details. Because high-quality goods require a higher intensity of labor, they generally cost more.

If money were no object I'd say go for the best quality at all times, period. But since money *is* a concern, I say go for it some of the time, where it really counts, with your investment buys—the basics and classics, those clothes and accessories that are going to be around the longest and that you wear the most. You can be somewhat less discriminating with the "latest thing," and/or incidental additions that can be easily and inexpensively replaced.

A high price tag and/or a designer label is usually a fairly good indicator of quality, but it's not a guarantee. These days in order to get the best deals you have to do your own quality checks. You need to be well equipped to recognize great quality when you see it—not only in order to cash in on bargains but also to know what slight quality alterations you can make yourself that will upgrade moderately priced clothes. Your best bet: Develop your own inner quality detector. We've already talked about fabric and design, so let's consider *workmanship* and some of the *quality finishes* that are the hallmarks of quality clothes.

1. In general the better a garment is made on the inside the better it will wear. Seams on the garment *and* on the lining should be straight and tightly sewn (the more stitches per inch, the sturdier the seam) with no pulls or puckering. Lining seams should be extrastrong in heavy coats. All edges should be finished. Seam allowance should be generous. Full linings should never fight the drape of the garment and in jackets and coats should always be stitched to the garment in key areas like shoulders, armholes, and sleeve hems to avoid snagging when putting on and taking off.

2. Zippers should work flawlessly, be the same color as the garment, and be neatly concealed in well-sewn plackets.

3. Buttons should be sewn on well and meet the buttonholes straight on. Buttonholes should be neatly finished with closely spaced stitches and no loose threads. Matching buttons should really match. If a fabric is heavy, as in coats and some jackets, the button should have a stem that is the length of the thickness of the garment material. Plastic reinforcement disks on the inside also help keep buttons on. If a fabric

is very delicate the underside of the spot where the button is attached should be reinforced with a small square of matching fabric and interlined with muslin if necessary.

4.  Bad hems cheapen any garment. Hemline stitching should be invisible. If the material is very delicate or transparent the edge should be finished with a hand-rolled hem. If you buy a garment with a poorly sewn hem it's a good idea to rehem it before you wear it.

5.  Expensive skirts and slacks should be fully lined with dyed-to-match silk or silk taffeta, if the garment fabric needs extra body. In suits the lining of the skirt and jacket should be made from the same fabric.

6.  Jacket shoulders should fit squarely; back vents and collars should lie flat and not pucker.

7.  Plaids and other patterns should match at the seams, collars, and pockets.

8.  Trouser and jacket pockets should be deep and roomy. There should be no rippling below or above the waist on straight skirts.

9.  Shoulder pads should be well shaped and attached with Velcro for easy adjustment or removal (except on delicate fabrics like silk).

Needless to say, all your clothes will not meet these high standards, but the ones you spend major money on should come as close as possible.

## COMFORT

Our *soeurs sportifs* illustrate the need for comfort and freedom of movement —another important *Dress Like a Million* tenet. As Yogi Berra might say, fashion becomes a pain when you're not comfortable.

Of course, our comfort zones are all different. Stiletto heels can be one woman's dream and another woman's nightmare. The trick is to really know the boundaries of *your own comfort zone* and put those boundaries right up there with your top fashion priorities. Make them nonnegotiable. My personal confort zone includes being able to get my hands into a pair of pockets, sit yoga style, and move around. I don't like to feel constricted—and probably never will. If you're comfortable in tight skirts that require crossed legs when sitting and make jumping over puddles an impossibility, that's fine. But don't wear something that *you* find uncomfortable just for fashion's sake. We have moved beyond that.

Ethnic finds can jazz up
simple basics—whether
they're as simple as a
Chinese vest and shoes,
African bangles, or
Mexican earrings.

## SMALL PLANET DRESSING

Borrowing fashion ideas from other cultures isn't exactly new. Designers have been doing it for years, and everybody and their sister had a collection of Indian scarves and knickknacks in the Woodstock/Haight-Ashbury years. But multicultural fashion ideas are even more accessible to the masses than before. High technology has made this a very small planet and it's getting smaller every day. It's my guess that we'll be borrowing more fashion bits and pieces from various worldwide ethnic groups and cultures as this decade progresses. Indonesian sarong-type skirts were around for a while; so were Scottish tartans and kilts. Then there were Spanish bolero jackets, African jewelry and kente cloth, West Indian silver bangles, and general global folklorico. And of course, our own ethnic American Indian look has a resurgence every other year.

So if ethnicity is your bag, keep your eyes peeled for inexpensive ethnic ideas and accessories—they're a great way to perk up simple wardrobes. (See Chapter 6.) And it's also bonding. We are, after all, the family of man.

# Cheap Frills

ACCESSORIES, ACCOUTREMENTS, AND ACCENTS

Accessories, contrary to their name, do a lot more than just accessorize; they allow you to move your basics into the realm of individual style. Accessories (or sometimes even the *deliberate* absence of them) add character and help shape and define your look. They can also act as champion rejuvenators. Drape a fabulous shawl over Mom's old long wool coat for extra warmth *and* style. A great Navajo concha belt turns ordinary jeans into a look from a Ralph Lauren ad, and simple but stunning oversized earrings totally shift the focus of a basic black dress. And like line, accessories can also redirect the eye—away from trouble spots.

The exact accessories you choose are really a matter of individual taste and style, but unless clutter is already a *successful* integral part of that personal style I strongly suggest keeping it simple. The old classic chic maxim "less is more" has already become the mantra of the nineties. Still, if piling on the accessories works for you—that is, if you've figured out some way to go into overload with style and grace, and that *is* your look—stick with it, absolutely. That is, after all, what personal style is all about.

Those rare exceptions aside, however, a single glitter, unusual twist, or splash of color will generally do the trick for most of us. A fashion editor friend with a hyperpenchant for accessories once told me that every morning just before she left the house she'd look in the mirror and take one thing off

—whether she thought she needed to or not. When in doubt, she advised, leave it out. And I agree.

That doesn't mean accessories have to be boring or even safe. Quite the contrary. Accessories are still one of the best ways to break loose, take some risks, and express yourself without going broke. I love what my sister the fashion mavin said when we were talking about the pros and cons of gold and silver Lurex. "There's nothing wrong with a slightly trashy accessory," she declared. "I think they're fun. . . . They're usually inexpensive and when you get bored with them you can throw them away."

Absolutely right. Experimenting with add-ons, unless you're into big-time Liz Taylor–type bijous, *is* generally much less of a high-stakes proposition than playing around with full alternative wardrobes. The bottom line is to simply tone down a peg and put a rein on excess. Major flash and gimcrackery are more eighties than nineties.

With accessories, as with clothes, the best plan is to acquire a few basic, versatile, and ideally unique, timeless pieces that are capable of adding interest and instant personal style to the simplest outfits year after year, and then augmenting that collection with the occasional new, whimsical, or maybe even slightly trendy pieces to keep your look updated and fresh. But it's important to note, as you'll see as you read on, that it's very often more *how* you wear a particular accessory than the piece itself that adds that unusual twist or shifts an outfit from serious to lighthearted—and vice versa. My friend Lulu, for instance, wears her signature strand of pearls even with T-shirts and tights, which definitely adds a touch of fancy to an ultracasual look.

Again, of course, any big money should go into items that offer style longevity, such as simple gold and silver jewelry, great leather belts, a fabulous shawl, etc. (See Chapter 5 for the principles of investment buying.) With that said, let's take a closer look at specific accessories—from the ground up.

## SHOES

Footwear, perhaps more than any other accessory in a pared-down wardrobe, has the ability to subtly shift the entire mood of an outfit and give it attitude. Picture, for instance, a simple white tailored shirt tucked into a pair of belted cotton khaki slacks. What kind of shoes would you wear with it? Loafers, sneakers, Birkenstocks, cowboy boots, desert boots, moccasins, Doc Martens, white bucks? All would theoretically work, but each presents a very different mood and attitude. Loafers are more East Coast prep; sneakers are sporty; Birkenstocks, hippyish; cowboy boots, western chic; Doc Martens, hip and cool; and desert boots, nonfashion-conscious intellectual. And how about white pumps? They would turn this classic casual outfit into a joke.

Your footwear not only *reflects* your personality but *effects* it too. Unlike a piece of jewelry or even a hat that you put on and forget about, shoes are an omnipresent influence. Even if they are so comfortable that you actually forget about them, you simply walk, feel, and act differently in different shoes. You would be a much tougher cookie in combat boots than you would be in ballet slipper flats. Your stride would be heavier, you'd feel more macho, and you'd probably even be able to lift more. So consider the way you *feel* in shoes as much as the way they look, and try to buy shoes that give you an emotional lift—as well as perhaps the physical one.

Regardless of what's in at the moment, you still can't go wrong with any of the classics and their variations: sneakers, loafers, espadrilles, ballet slipper flats, and simple flat sandals for casual wear; low-cut pumps, Gucci-type loafers, and Chanel-type slingbacks, for traditional career wear; and single-strap slingback sandals, pumps, or ballet slipper flats for dressy evenings.

But whatever style you choose watch the quality. Poor quality shoes bring down the tone of an outfit quicker than you can say Manolo Blahnik. Quality is most obvious in suede and leather shoes and boots, since cheap leather looks hard and brittle and the fine, expensive variety looks so sumptuous and butter soft you don't know whether to wear it or eat it. Top-quality leather shoes are worth what you have to pay for them—on sale, of course, whenever possible.

Casual canvas shoes, on the other hand, like espadrilles or Ked clones, don't last very long no matter what you spend for them. So keep your eyes peeled for cheapies that can look every bit as good as the costlier ones.

Thankfully it is no longer necessary to cripple our feet in the name of fashion, so unless you're horribly addicted to perilously high heels, forget about them. They make for pretty *Vogue* pictures and can be quite lovely for evening—especially if you're being chauffeured around—but they look positively passé and, well, even tarty during the day. Let's face it, high heels are primarily worn to make the leg look sexier, which in turn is supposed to attract the opposite sex. While it's true high heels can have a certain sexual allure, they also cause muscle spasms, bunions, calluses, shinsplints, corns, and throw your body's alignment totally out of whack. And as far as attracting the opposite sex goes, what kind of guy are you looking for? As far as I can tell real guys aren't impressed by someone who sacrifices health and comfort for vanity. Even if you are short and wear high heels for extra height, reconsider. A slim, tapered medium-high heel offers extra inches, grace, and a lot more style, and for casual wear you can always get a little lift from a thickish sole or *mini*platform. In this day and age comfort should be a priority not a bonus.

*Warning:* Ultrashort skirts and high heels are a deadly combination for anyone but a few twenty-one-year-old models or hookers. The older you are the more lethal the combination. Career women have the most to lose with this getup since stilettos and superminis seem to negate intellectual prowess. Also, it's difficult to take anyone very seriously when you can see her behind every time she bends over.

Aside from the comfort factor, your shoes should ideally look good on your feet, complement your legs, be in keeping with the mood of your clothing, and work well proportionately with your body type and outfit.

A *few tips*

- Shoes with straps across the instep or around the ankle are generally unflattering, since the straps interrupt the line of leg, making it appear shorter. The closer the shoe is to skin tone (or stocking tone), the less risky this design. (And the longer the leg, the less it matters.)
- Make sure the open toe on open-toed shoes is a good shape. If it allows only the big toe to sneak out or deforms the second toe as it squeezes its way into the open air, give the shoe a pass.
- Heavy, clunky heels are as outmoded as stilettos. If your legs are heavy this style will only make them look heavier. If your legs are slender you will look like Olive Oyl. And to add insult to injury they also encourage a clumsy gait. Pass.
- Ultradelicate shoe styles are also risky for heavy-legged women, since the contrast will emphasize the breadth of the leg.
- Watch color balance. Although black is basic it doesn't go with everything. It can look too heavy with light-toned clothes. White is tricky too. With the exception of Keds, ballet slipper flats, espadrilles, and other flat sporty styles, white shoes are a big mistake. Aside from making the foot look larger, white shoes are just plain tacky. As one self-described fashion critic plainly put it, "There is no reason for anyone, in any part of the world, to own a pair of white shoes, please!" Her primary fear is that some women might think that wearing white shoes means they have to match it with, horror of horrors, a white purse, which she considers to be the ultimate assault on taste. "There is no white bag," she asserts, "that doesn't look like plastic, even if it's a three hundred dollar Chanel with leather running through the gold chain strap. . . . If someone feels they have to have a white bag, which

some people in Florida probably do, buy a navy bag with white trim, or a light taupe bag with white trim." Good idea.

The windup: Beige-toned shoes are almost always a better choice than white. Your best bet, of course, is to simply follow the suggested color plan in Chapter 3 and look for tones that complement your base neutral. They will go with everything. Shoes in accent colors can be fun, but they're a luxury. Again, get your basics first.

- Watch texture balance. Garments of heavy textured fabrics like wool need to be balanced with a heavier shoe, which is why tweeds look perfect with English walking shoes (and variations). Gauzy summer dresses, on the other hand, call for a more delicate shoe.
- A low-cut pump or a low-cut slingback with a low-to-medium narrowish heel are very flattering designs for most women. Tapered toes (as opposed to rounded ones) make the foot look slimmer but are generally less comfortable.
- Women with big feet need to pay particular attention to the cut of their shoes. Best bets: shoes that are cut to the foot without an extended sole showing around the edges, and ones made of thin leather.
- Skinny ankles look best in low-cut shoes.
- Pants tucked into high boots cossack-style is not a good look—and frankly never was.
- A general rule of thumb for dressy shoes: The less shoe the better the leg will look.

The exception to all this excellent advice is when and if you are into bas couture, that is, dressing purposely askew. Then you can ignore all the tenets of proportion and good taste and just go for it. Doc Martens, those thick cushy-soled oxfords that a lot of the kids are wearing, are not a particularly flattering style proportionwise, but they can work with certain outfits if you've got the right look *and* the *right attitude*. I have to admit that even I sometimes give fashion a holiday and wear high-water pants (midcalf) with little white cotton anklets and sneakers, which, because my legs are pitifully skinny, is neither a brilliant proportional choice nor particularly complementary. But what can I tell you? I like it anyway. It's a relatively harmless fashion transgression, and Karl Lagerfeld *did* say somewhere that "the nineties are about doing what you want to do."

As to the latest shoe styles: They can be an excellent way to update and/ or add a little pizzazz to a relatively classic wardrobe—if, of course, they're compatible with your personal style. Here's the only snag with trendy shoes:

Since they're in today and out tomorrow you don't want to spend a fortune on them. On the other hand, you don't want to buy cheap imitations either —because they will look just that. So if the trend is, say hypothetically, multicolored high-topped sneakers that sell for $25, great. Splurge if you love them. But if the trend is motorcycle boots, and good ones cost $250, forget about them—unless, of course, you're a bike messenger and can get infinite wear out of them.

Boots are crossover shoes these days. That is, they're more than just footwear for those extracold winter days. A good pair of classically designed, top-quality boots is definitely a worthy investment—especially if you live in a four-season climate, but they can be terribly expensive. So take extra caution in avoiding easily outdated styles. A slim silhouette, modified toe (neither too round nor too tapered), and flatish heel are the hallmarks of classic boots. I was looking through my first book, *Womanstyle,* which was published in 1979, and almost all of the Susan Bennis Warren Edwards boots pictured there would still be winners today. So we are definitely talking long-term investment here.

Are cowboy boots a viable option? No, if you work in a conservative environment and can only afford one pair of boots. Yes, definitely, if they don't squeeze your toes and you live in the West. And yes again if they are an integral part of your style and you were wearing them before they were shown with short froufrou skirts in *Vogue.* In other words—if you were country when country wasn't cool. The good ones cost. Don't invest hard-earned money if you don't feel totally natural in them and have the opportunity to wear them a lot.

*My personal thoughts on other current trends:*
- Cowboy half boots are basically cowboy boots that have been amputated at the ankle. They award Western cachet without the inconvenience of having to jiggle your pant hems over bothersome boot tops every time you stand up. A sound idea. They are trendy but can work with jeans and even slim-line slacks if you're the pioneering type. With skirts, though, they cross the line from trendy to tasteless.
- Oxfords plus are essentially sized-down clones of men's standard tie-up shoes—Doc Martens included. They look so practical that I rather like them. But they really are best with slouchy tailored suits with a slight masculine edge . . . or maybe jeans or chinos.
- Mules—I love them in the seraglio. Sorry, but I grew up in Miami, and for me they will always be synonymous with gold pedal pushers and cat-eyed rhinestone sunglasses. Personally if I'm going to flip-flop

around I'd rather do it in rubber thongs. (This is probably known in psychojargon as "negative nostalgic association.")

- Platforms—I already did them in the seventies and quite enjoyed being three inches taller then. So I would almost be tempted to try a sensible *miniplatform*. The problem is they can look very bizarre on skinny legs in skirts, and I would have to rehem all my pants. So I personally am passing on this fad. Your call. If you do decide to try them, though, you might want to think about carrying an emergency Ace ankle bandage in your bag—just in case.

- Clogs: Sure. They are, after all, classics in Scandinavia and fun to knock around in on weekends. Whatever you do, though, don't take them seriously. I like them best in the garden and on teenagers.

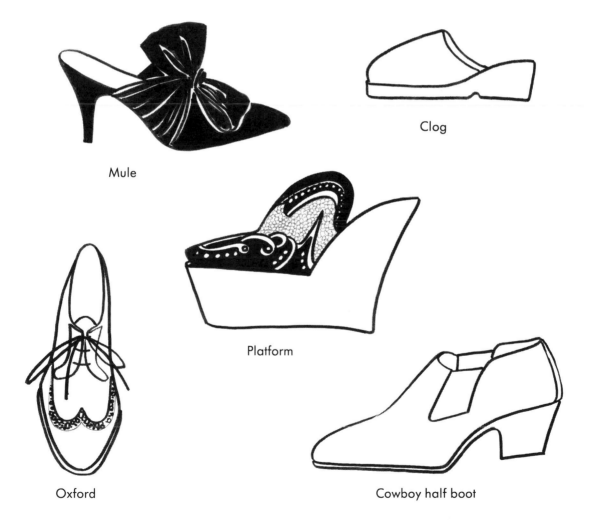

Mule

Clog

Oxford

Platform

Cowboy half boot

*One last tip:* Check with a shoe repair before tossing out quality shoes with minor faults. I've been told that a good shoe repair can shorten a heel a quarter of an inch to a full inch, and can replace overly thick or narrow heels with more suitable ones. They can also cut off straps and make shoes a tad wider.

*And one last warning:* Shoes can be addictive. Ask Imelda. Before you get carried away figure out what you really *need.* If you're a traditional career woman, two to four pairs of shoes should do the trick for work, and unless you are wined and dined every evening, one or two pairs of dressy shoes should prove quite adequate. For play, a couple of pairs of sneakers or loafers. Remember, it's ultimately more chic to wear the same pair of glorious top-quality shoes every day than a different pair of mediocre ones every other. On the other hand, if you find irresistible ones on sale . . .

## HOSIERY

In a conservative environment the general rule of thumb is to wear sheer panty hose in a neutral tone that makes your legs look ever so slightly tanned. Black skirts, though, also look terrific with black- or gray-tinted hose. Sheer patterned stockings—with little dots, triangles, or flowers— and sheer colored tints, generally make the leg look slightly diseased and should be avoided, as should black fishnet stockings, which are best relegated to the Kit Kat Klub.

White stockings basically look best on nurses. If you're not in the medical profession don't bother with them. They make the leg look heavier, and they have a semipuritanical, unsexy edge to them. As my very astute friend Ronnie pointed out, "Most people's skin turns that ashy stocking white just before it turns green and they die."

You might actually want to rethink your panty-hose habit this decade. Panty hose are invaluable in winter for extra warmth. They do add polish and finish to an elegant ensemble and are practically de rigueur in a traditional office environment. But with casual wear in the heat of summer? If you've got good legs and a slight tan it's perfectly OK to give them a miss.

*Some other tips:*
- In general the sportier the shoe the more opaque the hose it can take. The dressier the shoe, the more sheer the stocking.
- When buying panty hose the best way to test color is to hold them up against your inner forearm rather than the back of your hand, which is usually darker than your legs (except perhaps in the middle of summer).

- Tights are great in winter for extra warmth. They look especially terrific on a great pair of legs with a short skirt. They look awful with high heels. The most goof-proof color balance method is to keep tights the same color, or at least the same value, as shoes and skirt. Legs will look longer when tights and shoes match.

Socks are a great way to create fun, specialized looks on a shoestring. For example: White socks and flat leather sandals have a certain European schoolgirl flair. White anklets and Keds have a sort of practical, unstudied, girl-next-door appeal. Argyles and loafers mix well with tweeds and flannels for a classic campus look. Heavy wool socks are great rolled over the top of hiking boots, and white anklets worn with heels is, well, uh, a specialized look. Needless to say, none of these inspirations are recommended for a conservative office.

A *great tip:* Wool or acrylic leg warmers are indispensable in miserable cold winters when you have to wear skirts to work. They slip easily over stockings and keep your legs toasty warm until you get to the office where you can whip them off in about a second. It's even a good look when you get them in the same color as your coat.

## BAGS

Since a bag is something you use every day, don't skimp. A good bag is an investment buy that will last for years. Your basic everyday bag should be in a color that blends in nicely with your base neutral, in a style that is totally in tune with your needs, and in a design that you'd be proud to set down in the middle of a table in the best restaurant in town (not that you necessarily would).

The basic style is pretty much dictated by your life-style. Obviously a clutch would be less than an ideal choice for a mother of four adolescents, whereas it would be perfect for a CEO who could pop it in her briefcase for ultimate consolidation. Convenience is the bottom line. Some of us require bags that are roomier, sturdier, more lightweight, with more compartments, etc., than others. Practicality is of the utmost importance. So before you buy your next bag consider what you generally carry, what kind of closure would work for you, and what kind of straps or handles make the most sense for you.

But your bag should also add a dash of style to your look. So it should be ultimately compatible with your clothes, personality, and body type. If your fashion approach is soft and relaxed, a lightweight, soft leather or suede pouch might be a good choice. A crisper tailored image calls for a more structured geometric shape. And a heavy-gauge nylon or canvas fishing-type bag, or even a chic knapsack could add panache to a casual sporty look.

Aside from your everyday bag you'll need a quality bag or two for dressy affairs and some sort of fun pouch for casual evenings out when you don't want to lug around your daytime bag. Again, they should be in keeping with your personal style.

*Other tips:*

- The size of your bag should be in sync with your size. Too large a bag on a small woman looks as misproportioned as a tiny purse on a large woman. If you're petite but need a roomy bag try the soft-sided expandable variety. Also watch the length of your shoulder bag strap. If it's too long, (say, it hangs below your hip) get it shortened at a shoe repair shop.
- The days of matching shoes and bags are long gone. As long as your shoe and bag colors blend and don't clash outright you're fine.
- Comparison shop for quality. Examine bags by Hermès, Gucci, Chanel, etc., then look for less costly renditions, and watch for these quality checkpoints:

Leather bags made from top-grain leather are stronger and more durable than those made from split leather. Since good leather absorbs oil, one expert suggests rubbing your finger on your forehead then running it along the bottom of the bag in question. The best leathers, she says, won't show the oil.
Good lining makes for longer wear. Leather is the most durable liner; cotton and nylon are the lightest weight.
Straps should be double sided with no loose threads.
Seams should be piped or bound for ultimate strength.

One last thing: Knapsacks, which I raved about in my first book for their practicality and comfort, have finally been sanctioned into official fashiondom as I predicted they would be in my first book. (I love when that happens.) Even Gucci is selling them like hotcakes. If you do a lot of walking, carry a lot in your bag, and one shoulder has slipped slightly lower than the other due to years of heavy toting, now would be the perfect time to give knapsacks a chance. Since the weight is evenly distributed on your back, you hardly notice it—there's no strain or discomfort. When your load is light or your coat is too heavy to conveniently slip the backpack on and off, simply sling it over one shoulder.

Drawback: The corporate world is probably not quite ready for the knapsack yet. Give them another three to four years.

*Warning:* Don't keep valuables in outside knapsack pockets, and move the bag to your front in especially crowded areas or especially risky places like New York subways and downtown Rio.

## JEWELRY

There are essentially two schools of thought on jewelry that fit nicely into the nineties' niche. One is to collect a few precious and treasured items, perhaps with some sentimental value attached, that make you happy every time you look at them and that you can wear with everything. These become your signature pieces. This is a great plan for women with very defined senses of style. Our stylish friend, retail whiz Gayle Shulman, is a major exponent of this first approach. Here's how she handles it—as only she can tell it.

> I wear all the same jewelry every day. The few things I have are good and I wear them all the time. I leave all my rings on at night. Maybe once a month I take them off and let my fingers air out. I have three bracelets that I wear on my left hand—two gold, one silver. I never take them off. I sleep, swim, and bathe with them. They're real, they're there, they're part of me. They jingle-jangle, I like it. I have a series of chains I wear. I take them off at night because they're long. I have one short chain with a pair of gold lips on it that was my honeymoon present, which doesn't even have a clasp, so it's on for good. I have a couple pairs of earrings; I have my diamond studs, which I wear every day and sleep in, and a beautiful pair of large gold earrings that I bought myself as a present on a trip a few years ago. Then I have a few pieces of costume jewelry—either crystal or brass and turquoise—not junk, real something.

There you have it—the epitome of plan A.

The second way to go is to continually play and experiment with relatively inexpensive fun, new, costume jewelry, which involves quite a lot of shopping time and genuine fashion interest. Or you could play a combination of plan A and B, which is probably your best bet. Start out with a few solid investment pieces (that you can eventually pass along to your grandchildren) and supplement them with the occasional whimsical piece when you happen upon it—and can afford it.

Every wardrobe profits from a few good jewelry investment pieces like these.

Earrings should suit your face and stature. Big earrings like these call for a strong face.

Ex-covergirl New York restaurateur *extraordinaire* Barbara Smith works the combination plan with total finesse. She has her few favorite investment pieces in silver and gold—a couple of great watches, large but simple bracelets, and big earrings—that she's been wearing for years. "Gold and silver," she happily points out, "are forever." But she's also a big costume jewelry aficionado and is always on the lookout for "great costume jewelry that doesn't cost a lot."

"My style really is the jewelry I wear," says Barbara, "and it almost always makes a statement. It's important for me in the restaurant business to always look different. That's where the costume jewelry comes in. I wear basic colors like black, navy, and red, and then just dress them up. I tend to wear the jewelry that other people won't buy because it's almost too far-out. I may wear one earring that's very long and one that's short, or very large jewelry. I love rhinestones—they're the best. They just glitz everything up. When I walk into the room I like everybody to know B. Smith has arrived."

And they do. Barbara's personal style is a perfect topping for her natural beauty. She has a great face for big earrings (wide, open, and gorgeous, with a smile to challenge Tom Cruise's). She keeps her hair very short and "wears her face." She feels her earrings brighten up her face and, as she puts it, "take it in whatever direction I want it to go." And she wisely stays away from necklaces that would only compete with her earrings. She simply doesn't need them.

Regardless of what approach you take, there's no doubt that a few good timeless investment pieces will stand you in good stead a good way into the next century. If you're a classic dresser, worthy investments might include a few fabulous gold and/or silver chains that could be worn together, a string of pearls, or diamond studs. If you're into a more ethnic approach the aforementioned concha belt, gold African bangles, superlarge solid hoop earrings, or some replica of an antiquity classic from the shop at the Natural Museum of Art, would pass the investment muster, and so on. The main thing with any investment jewelry is that it totally complements your style and that you are mad for it. Hopefully it is also versatile. Aside from the fact that a piece of good jewelry lasts forever and that you could always sell it under extreme financial duress, it tends to upgrade the look of everything else you're wearing.

What if you don't already own those few great pieces and you're not yet in the cash position to buy the real thing? Simply buy a few imitation classics and/or concentrate on good quality costume jewelry for now. Costume jewelry that is well designed and proclaims itself costume jewelry can be wonderful. Stick to natural materials like wood, stone, copper, straw, coral, jade, turquoise, etc., and stay away from poorly designed tinny pieces that try to look like real jewelry but fail miserably.

If you opt for gold-plated replicas buy quality and keep it simple. Make sure the color is not brassy, and avoid any flashy styles that would cost a mint if they were made of solid gold—much too obvious. It's also perfectly OK to mix real gold and silver with quality imitations. Wear a real gold Rolex watch, for instance, and nobody would dare question the pedigree of your two imitation gold neck chains.

There is some excellent gold look-alike jewelry in the stores these days. I was recently scouting the stores for a pair of classic gold hoop earrings (about 1½ inch diameter). The 14 carat gold ones I liked were $170. A perfect facsimile (Monet) in faux gold was $24. Since my saintly saleslady told me all the gold jewelry would be 50 percent off the following week, I decided to wait for the real thing, but meanwhile, the imitations were so good, I bought a pair anyway—perfect for vacations and any iffy travel situations.

Other pearls of wisdom:

- *Bangle bracelets* usually call for multiples. One skinny bangle by itself tends to look lonesome and pathetic. Bangles are mostly designed for "normal" size wrists consigning small-wristed women like myself to shop in teen departments and/or buy the hinged variety. Although I love the look of bangles on other women I've never had much luck finding perfect ones for myself.
- *Watches:* Get a good one—or two. Thanks to quartz and the miniaturization of printed circuitry there are a lot of great-looking inexpensive watches to choose from these days—and they're usually accurate to the microsecond. Again, the trick is simplicity—and comparison. First look at expensive, simply designed, quality watches like the Cartier tank or a Christian Dior design. Then look for the knockoffs. I bought my husband a wonderful ultrathin watch with a black crocodile band that was as handsome as any Cartier—jewel-tipped stem crown and all—for only $39.95. I loved it so much I went back and bought myself one. I replaced the black band with a smaller natural pigskin band (another $25). It looks like a $500 watch—so I've been told anyway.
- *Earrings* must suit your face to look good. Most small faces are overpowered by big bold earrings, and strong faces call for strong earrings.

  Also beware of earrings that are the same color as your hair or that blend in with your skin or collar. You might think that because the color of a pair of earrings matches your hair or clothes well that they are the perfect choice, but in fact when they match too well they just disappear. I once bought some jet-black earrings and learned the hard way.

- Don't let any jewelry overwhelm you. Keep jewelry scaled to your size. Heavy women should avoid chunky, bulky beads and pendants. Flat is better.
- You can use certain pieces of jewelry to help create a line or correct an existing one. If, for example, the buttons on a favorite blouse are awkwardly spaced so that two buttons undone makes the neckline too high, and three left unbuttoned is too revealing, you could use a tie tack, a delicate pierced earring, or a small pin as a makeshift in-between button. Or you could wear a string of pearls or beads knotted to fall between the second and third button of the blouse.
- Use jewelry pieces creatively. Sometimes jewelry works just as well for purposes for which it was not originally designed, like the aforementioned tie tack button. Other ideas: An old ring can be used as a scarf loop, an antique cufflink can be transformed into a lapel buttonhole filler, a clip-on earring can hold a scarf in place. Don't be afraid to take things out of context.

Meanwhile keep your eyes peeled for bargains in thrift stores and at auctions and sales, and remember, you don't really *need* a lot of jewelry.

## BELTS

Belts are terrific. They can perk up boring outfits, update old classics, add color and/or texture, and totally shift the shape, proportion, drape, and style of an ensemble. They can also hold your pants up, although that's usually secondary these days.

The width of the belts you choose depends primarily on your body type.

- Tall thin women can wear almost any type of belt.
- Short women usually do best with narrow belts. In general, the smaller you are, the narrower the belt.
- Heavy women should steer clear of wide belts, but need not forgo them altogether. Whatever the belt don't cinch it too tightly. (See Chapter 2.)

Belts are invaluable wardrobe staples, and good ones can last a decade or more. But don't spend huge amounts of money on novelty styles.

Our friend Gayle, whose latest uniform is a long skirt, camisole, and roomy overblouse, wears a narrowish belt slung low on her belly and drapes the blouse over it. When she found a belt she liked she called the manufacturer and asked if he could make her two belts a foot longer so she could loop them around twice and let them hang a bit. "You could never buy those belts in the store," says Gayle. "I invented it because I wanted that look and I had to make it for myself." The moral: If you can't find what you want, think about ways to make it or get it made.

If you're short waisted you can use narrowish belts like Gayle does to visually drop the waist. Wear them slung low or just loosely buckled so that they vee slightly in the front. Contour belts that dip below your waistline are a natural. And another instant waist lowerer is one of my favorite belts —the wide elastic style that you can easily slip down right over the top of your hips. Long-waisted women can go for wider belts, but should match the belt and pants color to keep legs from looking shorter. (See Chapter 2.) Contrasting colored belts emphasize and bring attention to the waistline, so avoid them if your waist and/or hips are full.

If you are an ardent belt wearer, wonderful interchangeable belt buckles are great investments. It's a "twofer"—you get both jewelry and a belt for the price of one. You can find terrific buckles at specialty stores, antique stores, second-hand shops, western stores, and sometimes even at auctions. Most belts can be adapted for buckle changes by a good shoe repair shop. Remember, though, that if you are wearing an important buckle, that is, one that makes a statement in and of itself, you don't need to wear a lot of other jewelry with it. Earrings are fine, but big bracelets are usually a risk, since they're in the same area as the belt when you lower your arms.

A lot of low- to medium-priced slacks, skirts, and dresses come with tacky imitation leather belts. Get rid of them. They immediately downgrade any garment. Give them to your daughter or a neighbor's child who likes to play dress up—or recycle them. I recently used one to tie up a piece of canvas for storage. Ultimate recycling.

As for cost—as always, use common sense. Don't spend a lot on novelty belts, but good belts are excellent investments. If you find an incredibly handsome, unique, finely crafted tan leather belt that blends with almost everything in your beige-based wardrobe and is the perfect style for your figure, save up your money and buy it. You'll wear it for years and years.

## SCARVES AND SHAWLS

Scarves are a great, relatively inexpensive way to add interest or a splash of color. They can also change the line of a collar, soften an especially tailored look, help draw attention away from figure flaws, and rejuvenate golden oldies. But to work well in today's fashion arena scarves have to look and feel *completely natural.* So your best bet is to wear them in an easy way that requires minor fidgeting and readjustment.

The most versatile and easy-to-wear scarves are lightweight, long oblongs. You can hang them over or under jackets, knot them high or low, twist a few around your neck for an instant cowl-neck effect, slide a scarf ring (or small circular clip-on earring) on and up for an easternized bolo look, or wear narrow ones tied into a soft floppy bow under a collar.

I recently rediscovered an old, long black silk charmeuse scarf that I had completely forgotten about in the back of my armoire. Now I can't see how I got along without it. When I wear it under my black blazer, even with a T-shirt, the whole outfit immediately looks classier. It seems to fill out the look and add another lusher dimension. It's layering at its easiest.

While layering monotones adds lushness and clever mixing of prints adds sophistication, colorful scarves come in especially handy when the color of your top isn't particularly flattering. I used to have an old olive army fatigue jacket that I liked to knock around in on weekends even though olive brought out the worst in my skin tone. So I simply swathed my neck in a long red scarf which immediately perked up my complexion.

Aside from oblongs, scarves, of course, also come in various size squares and triangles. Larger scarves are usually more effective and versatile. Chiffon is probably one of the least bulky scarf fabrics and definitely one of the easiest to work with.

Here are some terrific easy-to-wear ways to tie scarves (compliments of the Fashion Accessories Association). Experiment with them to see which suits you the best—and don't be afraid to play around and try to come up with some of your own variations on these themes.

*The square knot/shoulder wrap:*
1. Fold a square scarf into a triangle. Flip one end over the other.
2. Take the upper end around and behind the lower.
3. Pull through and tighten.

Knot can be at your front, side, back, or on one shoulder. For a shoulder wrap, tie the knot in the front and pull the sides down over your shoulders.

*The bib wrap cowl:*
1. Fold a large square scarf into a triangle. Place the point in front.
2. Cross ends behind the neck.
3. Tie ends in front with a square knot.
4. For a cowl effect, take the center fold of the scarf and bring it over the knot, tucking the points into the neckline.

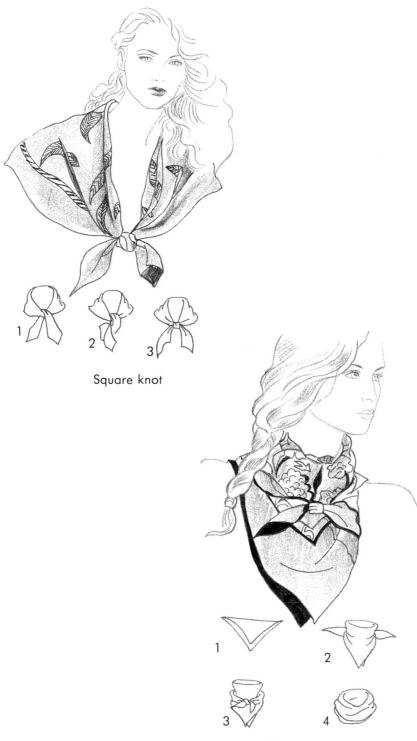

Square knot

Bib-wrap cowl

*Hacking knot:*

1. Fold an oblong scarf into half lengthwise.
2. Place around the neck and pull the two ends through the center fold.
3. Tighten the scarf to the side of the neck.
4. Form a bow.

Hacking knot

*Multiscarf wrap:*

1. Use two oblong scarves. Twist each into a loose coil.
2. Wrap the two coils around each other.
3. Wrap scarves around the neck in a cowl. Loosely tie the ends and tuck under or leave hanging.

Multiscarf wrap

*Men's tie/slip knot:*

1. Place an oblong scarf around the neck with one end longer than the other. Tie a single knot in the longer end.
2. Place the other end into and through the knot and tighten slightly.

Men's tie

*Faux bow:*

1 Make a loose knot in the center of an oblong scarf. Place knot under chin.
2. Cross ends behind the neck and bring them back to the front.
3. Place the ends through the knot going in opposite directions.
4. Tighten knot slightly.

Faux bow

*Ascot:*

1. Fold a square scarf into an oblong or use an oblong scarf.
2. Place around the neck and flip one end over the other.
3. For a traditional look tuck the ends into your shirt or jacket. For a more informal effect, move the fold to the side.

Ascot

Extralarge scarves move into the realm of *shawls,* which are generally made of soft drapable fabrics such as wool challis, silk, and cashmere. The softer and more drapable they are the better they'll look. Shawls are wonderfully practical since they pack like a dream and provide an extra layer of stylish warmth. And they are terrific rejuvenators.

- Drape a shawl over a wool coat for a totally new look. Either drape in the center with equal lengths on each side, or leave one side longer and fling the longer side across your body onto the opposite shoulder.
- Wear with suits and jackets instead of an overcoat when the weather is amenable. You can revive old jackets by simply tossing a shawl over outmoded lapels—or even tying the shawl in a loose knot in front of the lapels.
- A white or natural-color summer shawl is great for instant chic as well as ready protection from overactive air-conditioners.

Only two warnings with shawls:

1. Remember proportion; a large blanket shawl can overwhelm a small woman.
2. Think twice about overfringed styles. They're a bit too gypsyish and Haight-Ashbury.

## HATS

There are hat people and there are no-hat people. Hat people put on hats as nonchalantly as they would a pair of socks and feel totally comfortable and natural in them. No-hat people either look too studiously put together or feel so self-conscious that they end up taking their hats off less than an hour after they put them on. Or they simply don't think about hats at all.

If you are a hat person by all means go ahead and wear them. They certainly can add wit to your look, and they make for a very definitive style. But take heed: If you are going to wear anything other than an inconspicuous winter warmer, be prepared to be noticed. The bottom line: If you're not in the mood for comments, you're not in the mood for a hat.

*Three more tips:*
- There should be a genuine harmony between your hat and your personality.
- Hat shape must be complimentary to body and face shape. Small women should watch they are not overpowered by extrawide brims. Large women should beware of high crowns.
- Check hats from all angles when buying. It should look as good going as coming.

## GLOVES

The way I see it, it's about time for gloves to stage a comeback. They haven't been a really important accessory since the early sixties when little white gloves were still de rigueur, and as we all know, in fashion what goes around comes around. So prewarned is prearmed.

Meanwhile, gloves are wonderfully practical, if not indispensable, when the temperature drops. If you live in a cold climate silk- or cashmere-lined kid gloves could be considered a solid investment buy. As for color, you can't go wrong in a neutral tone that blends with your base neutral, but to add a little pizzazz you might consider a bright color, say red, to wear with your black-and-white Harris tweed coat. Gloves are inexpensive enough that you can get a few pairs and have a little fun. Before you make any purchases though, check some of the less tony department stores and discount shops in your area for real deals. I've found some terrific buys on bright gloves at stores like Alexander's (unfortunately, now defunct) in New York, and Ross Dress for Less in Los Angeles—neither particularly known for their chic. Look for gloves that fit perfectly and give the hand a slim silhouette.

*Other ideas:*

- Cashmere gloves are usually less expensive than leather and are a good standby for casual wear.
- If you have small hands shop at the beginning of the season when the shipments first arrive.
- In truly horrendous weather—like winter in North Dakota—forget about fashion and head to the ski shops for thermal skiing gloves. Down-filled mittens are probably warmest of all.

## LINGERIE

Underwear, as the name suggests, was originally designed to be worn *under* clothes—mainly for support and modesty. Today underwear is out of the boudoir, out of control, and being proclaimed as the ultimate accessory. Underwear as outerwear has been an ongoing trend for some time now, and it's hard to predict just when it's going to run its course, especially when such classy designers as Donna Karan lend the look authenticity by showing black lace bras peeking out from pin-striped suits. First we burn them, now we flaunt them. What is this world coming to?

We probably have Madonna and maverick designer Jean-Paul Gaultier to thank—or blame, depending on your predilection—for bringing bras and slips out of the closet and reinstating the bustier as la mode. Both were more out to shock the petite bourgeoisie than to hammer home a new fashion, but the naughty look caught on with the MTV crowd and then filtered down in a kinder and gentler version into mainstream fashion. But any way you look at it lingerie these days has taken on a whole new dimension.

The question is should you avail yourself of it. That all goes back to what we were discussing in Chapter 1—what do you want your clothes to say about you? If you want your fashion to reflect refined taste and elegance you'll probably want to forgo see-through blouses atop black lace bras—discretion being the better part of class. But if you're out for an overtly sexy image and have the body and personality to carry it off, a bustier may be just your cup of tea. But a warning: You're also going to need an exquisite fashion sense. Cutting-edge trends like this one straddle the line between tacky and tasty and require a strong sense of style to carry off. If your personal style is still in the budding stages, leave this look to the old pros. And need I say that regardless of latest styles or magazine ads, visible lingerie is still not a great idea for the office.

The bottom line to taking advantage of the underwear-as-outerwear trend is subtlety. Now that we know we *can* do it we can back off a bit. It has always been more alluring to leave something to the imagination. An open silk blouse worn over a silk and lace camisole is classier and just as sexy as an open blouse over a lacy bra. In general, I have to admit that I personally find bustiers and exposed bras rather junior. It's a fun look on teenagers and models, but it's kind of pointless on real women. Camisoles and body suits on the other hand, are winners for any age group.

As to underwear's original purpose, we all know that what we wear under our clothes makes a difference. Some of us need more support than others, and all of us need to pay attention to things like wearing flesh-toned lingerie under white, lightweight, sheer, or gauzy fabrics, and avoiding obvious panty lines.

A few other quick but pertinent reminders:

- With short skirts please don't wear panty hose with obvious thigh top reinforcement. It looks ghastly to see a line across the thigh when you sit down. Look for panty hose with bikini tops.
- It's totally anachronistic to see big loose breasts jiggling under a T-shirt, even when paired with Birkenstocks. (Check Chapter 2 for bra tips for your body type.)
- If you think you need a tight girdle or Lycra half-slip under a tight skirt chances are you shouldn't be wearing a tight skirt.

Since nighties and other sleepy-time wear go by the same proportion, color, line, and texture rules as daytime clothes, I'll leave you to your own devices here, but I do want to share a recent discovery: my husband's flannel pajamas. I bought him a pair for Christmas in a subtle blue-and-black plaid, which he swears he loves but never wears. (He still prefers a T-shirt or nothing—a real guy.) I love them for hanging around. I wear the bottoms (baggy and belted) with a black sweatshirt and Keds, and the top over a T-shirt, sort of like a shirt jacket. They are totally comfortable and cozy. That's my *personal contribution* to lingerie as outerwear.

## MISCELLANEOUS ACCOUTREMENTS

### Glasses

In the last five years or so glasses have become a verified fashion accessory, probably because baby boomers are fast approaching the age when it's hard to read a menu without them. Also, a lot of movie stars wear them to look smarter.

Since glasses do sit right in the middle of your face and unquestionably affect your image they deserve some attention here. The three basic things to consider when choosing your glasses are (1) what do you want them to say about you, (2) your face shape, and (3) your base neutral color.

In a traditional, conservative office you'd obviously want your glasses to say intelligent, tasteful, and responsible. So thin tortoiseshell or dark frames would be safe. If the frames are delicate enough you could also get by with a subtle color.

In a looser more flexible workplace, say advertising or media-related fields, you'd probably want your glasses to say creative, innovative, and up-to-date. So you could be a bit bolder in your frame choice: brighter colors, thicker frames, more extreme shapes.

What if you work in a traditional field but in private life you're really a fun-loving, avant-garde extrovert? Get two pairs of glasses—one for work, and one for the "real you."

As for face shapes, the conventional wisdom is that opposites attract, meaning that squarish or angular-shaped frames would best complement round faces, and round frames would look best on square faces. And most shapes look good on oval faces. While this is technically true, you also want to stay somewhat in tune with the times. Round glasses are definitely more hip these days. So if you have a round face and don't want to look totally square—both literally and figuratively—just look for roundish glasses with a very slight angle to them.

Perhaps even more important than slight nuances of shape is proportion. You don't want your glasses to either overpower your face (à la Swifty Lazar) or look like a bandage across your eyes. In general glasses should cover one-third of your face.

And last but not least, think about your facial features. High bridges on glasses make noses look longer; low bridges will shorten the nose. Light-colored bridges make the eyes look farther apart; a dark color brings them closer together. And your frames should meet your brow line and conform to the general shape of your eyebrow.

### Sunglasses

Sunglasses are pretty much a necessity in these days of continuing ozone depletion. According to eye specialists the sun's ultraviolet rays are a leading cause of cataracts, as well as of the premature aging of the delicate skin around the eyes. So protect your eyes now and save yourself some serious unpleasantness later. Make sure the lenses are coated to block UV rays.

Fashionwise sunglasses can be slightly larger than indoor glasses, but otherwise all the aforementioned proportion information applies. Don't forget to take your sunglasses off when you head indoors lest you look like an aging movie star hiding behind her Foster-Grants.

## Wallets, Datebooks, and Luggage

Since you use your wallet and datebook every day, many many times a day, you owe it to yourself to buy quality. That doesn't necessarily mean $300 Gucci wallets and $165 Filofaxes, it just means quality leather, not plastic items. You can find excellent Filofax clones for around $60 and wonderful top-grade leather wallets for anywhere from $40 to $80. You can use them for years until they wear out. Even when they're well aged they present a much classier image than brand-new plastic. Think amortization again. In the long run, you'll probably pay less than a penny every time you use your wallet and datebook—and you will be proud, not embarrassed, to pull it out of your bag. Sounds like a bargain to me.

The same goes for briefcases. If you use it every day, buy the best.

As for luggage, buy good, simply designed, tasteful, moderately priced pieces in dark colors that won't show dirt or the results of the shoddy handling they are bound to get. It would be a pity, in fact, to send gorgeous expensive luggage through the torture chambers of most airlines. And let us not forget the distinct possibility that your bag could simply vanish altogether. Unless you pay extra baggage insurance prior to a flight, the reimbursement you get for lost luggage is negligible. So save the money you'd spend on matching Vuitton bags and take an extra vacation.

Modern travel requires lightweight, practical bags that are not too heavy to carry yourself when you can't find a porter—which is usually whenever you need one. Your best bet is probably a substantial-weight treated canvas in a neutral dark shade with natural leather trimming. One of my personal favorite styles is the convertible backpack. I carried a black one all over Asia and can swear by the convenience. It looks rather like an ordinary rectangular canvas bag, good enough to carry into any first class hotel, but when the going gets rough you can zip open the back and magically turn it into an instant, very usable backpack. I couldn't live without mine.

Leather bags can be beautiful, but the best are too heavy and too expensive. Parachute rip-stop nylon is the lightest weight luggage fabric available and is great for short trips when you're doing the toting, but clothes tend to wrinkle more easily in them on long trips and airlines sometimes make you sign a damage waiver if you check the bag.

Your luggage, of course, no longer has to be totally coordinated, but to be on the safe side of hippie-retro, styles should be similar in design detail and colors should blend well. Buy bags as you need them. Keep them simple and neutral colored, and you won't go wrong.

# CHAPTER 7

# Putting It All Together

Now it's time to put all this priceless information to use and actually start pulling together a wardrobe for yourself. Even though you never have "a thing to wear," you obviously own some clothes. So the first step is to determine what you have that's actually wearable and what's simply taking up valuable space. This is a necessary step, since you have to get rid of the old and make room for the new in both the literal and metaphysical sense. *Warning:* This could be an all-day proposition, especially if you're a pack rat, so you might want to make it a weekend project.

The best approach is take all your clothes out of your closet and drawers section by section and try each piece on individually. Toss all clothes with no redeeming value into an "absolute discard" pile on the floor. Stack "maybes" in a neater pile on the bed, and hang "keepers" back in an empty section of closet according to color and design—i.e., all black slacks together in the slacks section, all print skirts together in the skirt section, all white blouses together in the blouse section, etc., etc. Make another pile somewhere of pieces that need to be altered to be worn. Anything that goes back in the closet, drawers, or on shelves should be ready to rock and roll.

I know all this sounds tedious, but once you get into it it does become, well, mildly interesting anyway, and you'll probably find that some of those old closet relics work today in ways you might not have expected.

A case in point: As I was personally going through this process a few weeks ago (let it not be said I don't practice what I preach) I came across a short periwinkle cotton jersey skirt and matching top that I swear I hadn't touched in five years. Both pieces were in great condition since the outfit was never especially flattering and I never wore it much. I tried it on. The skirt fit fine and was fashionably short; the top was too skimpy and looked outdated. I tossed the skirt in my "maybe" pile; the top went into discards. After I was finished with the initial blitz I checked the "maybe" pile and my "keeper" tops to see what I had that would go with the skirt. Amazingly enough there was a big roomy semiretired long periwinkle overblouse that was practically the same color. I tried it on with the skirt and it looked great. The proportion was perfect when I left the blouse open over a tank top. So in effect I now have a new casual summer outfit.

The moral of the story is this: Look at each piece with a new eye and an open mind. Perhaps the last time you wore a particular blouse you were into long skirts and the blouse was too long or bulky. How would it look today with a much shorter skirt? Or maybe you have recently switched from short skirts to long, or from slim pants to fuller ones. Now would be the time to re-evaluate your old cropped tops. How would certain shirts look over camisoles? Can dresses be belted differently, worn over T-shirts, under cardigans or jackets? Look at the full potential of each piece and try putting pieces together in ways you might not have thought of originally. Again, to do this right you're going to have to actually *try on* all the various combinations, so give yourself time.

If there are certain garments that you like and are in good shape, but you simply don't know what to do with within the context of your present wardrobe, store them separately until you get your new wardrobe together. Then pull them out and give them a second try. They might come in handy.

NOTE: If you're planning to have a child, please see the pregnancy section in the next chapter before you throw anything away.

Cleaning out your closet should give you a much clearer picture of what you need to buy—which leads us very neatly into the subject of shopping. So before we go any further, a few shopping hints.

## HOW TO SHOP

Do any serious shopping on a high-energy day when you're feeling strong and vibrant and have plenty of time. Don't shop under the influence of PMS. Your hormones will tell you you're fat and ugly and nothing looks good on you, except maybe that $1,200 Calvin Klein in the corner. The worst time to shop is when you desperately need something to wear—like that night. Ninety-nine percent of the time you'll wind up settling, which is a bad idea, especially when you're laying out a lot of money.

Shop alone. I know we are herd animals and shopping can be a social event, but unless you already have a tremendously solid sense of your own style it's too easy to get led astray by shopping partners. Even the opinions of your most fashion-savvy friends are mirrored in their own image, and, as we all know by now, what's good for them might not be good for you. Also, because your friends love you they may hesitate to tell you when something you seem to love looks horrendous. Shopping alone forces you to explore your own tastes and to develop style judgment. It also allows you to take your time without feeling guilty about keeping someone waiting.

The riskiest of all shopping partners are probably your mother and your husband. Your mother sees you as who she wants you to be or who you were, not as you are. And your husband, if he's not in a rush to get back to the ball game on TV, will most likely have a difficult time visualizing how an ensemble would look with the right shoes or a different coif. Neither Mom nor Hubby, God bless them, will be able to offer particularly valuable assessments. I'm sure there are exceptions. Jayne Meadows, for instance, once told me that her husband, Steve Allen, actually buys a lot of her clothes for her. Can you imagine? Steve is a rare bird indeed.

The minute a saleslady tells you "It's the latest thing, everybody is wearing it," tune her out. Her scope of style and fashion is too generic—and probably commission oriented as well. You can bet she won't have your best interests at heart.

Shop by process of elimination. Now that you know the colors, textures, lines, and shapes that are best for you, don't waste your time checking out every piece of merchandise in the store. Zero in on color first, then check out the style and fabric. This is a particularly useful strategy in discount stores where the occasional gem is mixed in with *beaucoup* garbage. Cruise through, stop when you spot one of your colors, look, feel, and either try on or move on.

Once you've selected something to try on, take your time and trust your instincts. Don't buy something that's just OK because you don't think you'll find something better. Or if you do, make sure it's returnable. Frankly, I don't recommend shopping in stores with no-return policies. You should always have the option of bringing something back. You might fall in love with something in the very next store, or your new garment may simply not cut the muster when you get it home.

Know your stores. In large department stores learn which departments are compatible with your style and budget, and concentrate efforts there (after, of course, a swift comparison run through the designer sections). And don't forget to check out the men's departments for large tops, jackets, and even baggy pants. Small women should also scout the boys' departments.

In discount stores, learn where they keep the good stuff. In all stores, make friends with a salesclerk or two who can alert you to upcoming sales and put things on hold for you. My friend Ronnie, an inveterate sales shopper who has gotten more great deals at sales than anybody else on the planet, has made buddies of a few select salespeople in many of her favorite stores by sharing shopping sources, bringing in little goodies like Batman pins for their kids, or treating them to an occasional cappuccino at coffee break time. Now they call her the minute there's a great sale. "I just do tiny little things so they don't forget me," she explains. "And it makes me feel good too—to let them know that I'm willing to put myself out to share something." There's a lesson here.

Breeze through stores whenever you can, even for a quick ten to fifteen minute look-see. That way you'll always know what's on the market and you can watch to see when something you especially like goes on sale. It's also a good way to fine-tune your fashion eye.

Shop the sales and get there early. The best sales are traditionally after Thanksgiving, Christmas, and Memorial Day, although these days stores are in such dire straits that it seems like there are constant sales. If you have a charge account at department stores you'll usually get a card announcing a sale preview day.

Ronnie strongly advises getting to previews whenever possible. Here's how she works a sale (and remember this woman is a pro): "I go to the previews and check them out. If there's something I desperately want I'll either get it then or wait it out depending on the store. At Neiman-Marcus things usually don't go below the initial sale price. So if I see something great that's reduced from $700 to $320 or $275 and I can't live without it, I'll buy it then. But at Bullock's or Saks, things are sometimes marked down an extra 50 percent five or ten days after they first go on sale. So I'll take a gamble and wait. Of course, if I *desperately* need it, I'll buy it when I first see it on sale."

*Warning:* Beware of prices that are initially inflated to make markdowns look like irresistible bargains. Anything heavily reduced, say 35 percent to 50 percent, very early in the season is suspect. When in doubt comparison shop.

In general, the later in the season you buy, the bigger reductions you'll find. Retailers traditionally buy a few months ahead of season, which means that by the time the season (whichever season that may be) actually arrives they are already thinking about where to put the merchandise for the next season. To make room for the new they need to move out the old, and sales usually do the trick. That's why you find good bathing suits sales in the middle of July—and great ones at the end of August.

If you find a defect in a garment, whether it's on sale or not, don't be embarrassed to politely ask for an additional discount. You'll usually get it.

In small boutiques you can sometimes create your own bargains. If you think something is overpriced, tell the clerk how much you love it and ask for a reduction. What have you got to lose? My friend David is notorious for his moxie. He figures he gets instant markdowns 65 to 70 percent of the time.

Don't worry about the size. One company's size 8 is another manufacturer's size 12. Learn to judge a garment by looking at the garment first and the size second. This is a handy skill to have when shopping in discount stores where sizes are often mismarked and at secondhand and thrift shops.

Check store sale policies. Some shops, such as The Limited and Express, will refund the difference between your original purchase price and a new sale price. Say, for instance, you buy a $40 blouse in June, then notice it's been reduced to $25 in July. They'll be happy to give you a $15 refund if you bring in the item and the sales slip. Just think, you'd then have $15 found play money to buy something new. Life is good.

Some department stores offer a 10 percent discount on items bought the day you sign up for a new charge card. So wait until you're in the market for something particularly costly, like a leather jacket for instance, to open a charge. If you already have one, you could always take your husband along (just this once) and let him open his own charge. He'll probably never use it anyway since men hate to shop, and you'll get your 10 percent off, which could represent a nice saving.

## WHERE TO SHOP

Aside from obvious places like department stores, your prized local boutiques, and mall favorites like the Gap, Express, and The Limited (all of which carry great, sensibly priced merchandise), there are other shopping sources you may not have thought about, at least recently, that can be a boon for the budget conscious.

### Thrift Shops
### (Including Swap Meets and Secondhand Stores)

There are definitely great bargains to be found at thrift shops, especially those in classy neighborhoods and/or those run by society's pet charities. But after years of study I've concluded that great thrift shop shoppers are a different breed of animal. They enjoy the thrill of the hunt as much as the kill. There's nothing they like better than sorting and sifting through racks and piles of old mediocre clothing in search of that one fabulous treasure that has eluded mere mortals and that they always seem to find. If they were a movie pitch they would be Coco Chanel meets Indiana Jones meets the Great White Hunter.

Can you be a successful great thrift shop shopper? Yes, if you have the following qualities: an uncanny eye, patience, stamina, perseverance, and grit. No, if you walk into a thrift store and see only junk or are the type who would rather go hiking than shopping.

Thrift store and secondhand store shopping also requires a certain amount of luck and timing. Some days the cupboard will be absolutely bare; other days will produce a bonanza. A tip from the pros: Be consistent—you have to go all the time. Since I have to admit that I'm less than consistent —by a lot—I've rarely struck pay dirt, but I have friends who have practically given up shopping at regular retail sources in favor of places like the Salvation Army and Goodwill.

And they have found wonderful goodies:

- custom-made doeskin fringed jacket for $24 (plus $50 for slight alteration and complete relining)
- wide burgundy alligator belt for $3
- lightweight Lanvin jacket in a subtle khaki glen plaid for $12 (plus $50 for full restoration, including cleaning, spot reweaving, and altering)
- men's navy cashmere coat in great condition for $15 (plus $100 for alterations and new lining)
- double-breasted wool crepe blazer, almost brand-new for $15 (plus $50 to alter)
- black Italian crocodile pumps for $8 (according to the expert shopper involved these were $400 shoes)
- Donegal tweed hacking jacket for $20 (plus another $60 to have it patched up).
- classic black gabardine straight skirt with back kick pleat, fully lined, Yves Saint Laurent label for $5
- man's large Scottish cashmere sweater, Ballantyne label for $10 (plus $10 to reweave one tiny hole)
- long off-white silk boudoir robe, almost new for $15 (plus $4 for cleaning)

And there's more: paisley shawls, silk hankies, beaded handbags, hand-knit sweaters, etc., etc.

If your imagination is tweaked and you think you're ready to give second-hand clothing a try, here are a few more tips gathered from first-rate secondhand shoppers:

- Dress for the hunt. Proper attire: leotard, body suit, or facsimile that allows you to try on a garment instantaneously with or without a dressing room—modesty intact. Slip-on shoes are a must.
- Do a quick overall price check first. If vases, lamps, and frames are reasonable there's a good chance the jackets and coats will be too.
- Look for timeless designs in natural fabrics that are more classic than costumey.
- Only buy things in relatively good condition (or that can be *easily* repaired.) If the seat is shiny or beading is missing or there are perspiration stains give it a pass.
- Don't overlook out-of-the-way little drawers where you could find real tortoiseshell combs, paste jewelry, cuff links and the like. And always be on the lookout for great sets of antique and/or amusing buttons. You'd be surprised at how much chic you can add to a jacket or coat simply by replacing ordinary buttons with special ones.
- And once again check the men's racks for suits, jackets, and forties-style baggy pants.
- It's OK to gently haggle. You may not get anywhere but it's good practice for third world travel.

## Almost-new Stores

These are stores that take in barely worn clothes on consignment. Once the clothes are sold the original owner gets her cut—usually something like 50 percent of final sale price. The quality and condition of the clothes are generally a lot more consistent than standard thrift shop fare. Display and ambience are more like a boutique than a secondhand store. The only problem is that the prices generally are too. I've personally never seen particularly good deals at almost-new shops, but since pricing is totally up to the store owners there are bound to be wide discrepancies from one store to another. One friend did find an incredible classic Chanel suit in black wool with a floral silk lining—and in super condition  for only $67 at the Next-to-New in Salinas, California, which isn't exactly the fashion capital of the world. So it just might be worth checking out your local almost-news. If not to buy, then maybe to trade or sell them some of your old mistakes outright.

## Craft Fairs

Craft fairs are held all over the country, so watch your local paper to see when there's one near you. They are a great source for unique and unusual accessories. Among other things, you can usually find wonderful hand-loomed oblong scarves and shawls, all kinds of hand-crafted jewelry, small interesting pocketbooks, hand-knitted sweaters, and silk-screened tops. Prices aren't always cheap, but with cash in hand you can usually negotiate a bit—especially near the end of the last day. Don't forget that well-made, one-of-a-kind items that are designed for longevity and are totally you can be terrific investment buys.

## Designer Discount Stores

You can get great deals at stores like Loehmann's (Calvin Klein, Perry Ellis, et al.) and Designer Labels for Less (mid-priced designers like Carole Little, Jones New York, and Paul Stanley), that specialize in off-season, poor selling, or slightly irregular designer goods. But you really have to know your stuff, since the designer labels are often cut out. One of the things I never liked about Loehmann's, which now has about seventy stores across the country, is their tough return policy. They recently changed their absolute no-return mandate to a store credit if you return within seven days. That's better but not great. Also since you change in a huge room with a bunch of other women you inevitably wind up getting, or in my case, giving, unsolicited advice, which is distracting to say the least. Still, if you can stay focused, can recognize quality, and have done your homework and know prices of designer offerings in department stores, you can find bargains— especially in suits, jackets, and coats. At Loehmann's always check their Back Room, where the best (and priciest) designer wear is stashed.

## Outlet Malls

These are a relatively new phenomenon that are cropping up across the country. They're set up like a shopping center, but all the stores sell below retail cost. Merchandise runs the gamut from Dansk to Donna Karan. I personally have only visited a few in southern California and was generally underwhelmed. Merchandise was limited, and prices weren't that much below those at a good sale. My friend Ronnie, our resident hard-core shopper, wasn't that impressed either. She said her husband dropped her off at one outlet mall for an hour while he did a few errands and after twenty minutes she was sitting on a bench in the sun waiting for him. If Ronnie is actually sitting down when there are stores around to be shopped you *know* nothing special is happening. However, don't let this stop you from checking out outlet malls in your area. Just make sure you've done your homework first and have a good grip on normal retail prices so you can differentiate between a really good deal and no big deal. The word "outlet," or "clearance" either for that matter, doesn't *guarantee* bargains. Also check return policies and factor in driving time and gas costs. In the long run it could turn out you'd do just as well on sale days at department stores.

## *Department Store Clearance Centers*

These are the reserves where unsold merchandise from your favorite department store ends up when they have to move it out to make room for the new stuff. Clearance centers seem to pop up where you'd least expect them. In San Mateo, California, for instance (about one half hour from San Francisco), there's a store called Finale, which turns out to be I. Magnin's clearance center for all their nineteen stores. Who knew?

Neiman-Marcus sends old goodies from their twenty-nine stores to two clearance centers called Last Call. One is in Austin, Texas, the other in Wayne, New Jersey. Saks Fifth Avenue has two outlets, called The Clearance Store, one in Franklin Mills, Pennsylvania (near Philly), the other in Sawgrass Mills, Florida (near Fort Lauderdale.) Bullock's has entire clearance floors in their Lakewood, California (near Long Beach), and Grossmont, California (near San Diego), stores. And Nordstrom has sixteen stores called The Rack, mainly in the West (three on the East Coast), where sale merchandise is further marked down. These stores, though, also carry special purchase merchandise and some of their own products, so they're not exclusively clearance outlets.

I can't personally vouch for all these stores, but from what I've heard—from a few very reliable sources—there are definitely great bargains to be had at Finale. One friend of mine bought a $700 Armani cashmere jacket there for $150. And a friend of hers bought a Calvin Klein suit for $250—the jacket itself was originally $800. According to the store manager, already-reduced merchandise is marked down an additional 25 percent the minute they get it. The following month it goes down to 30 percent off, then 40 percent. There's always a constant flow of incoming merchandise, and *major* shipments arrive every six weeks. When I spoke to the manager she was expecting a shipment of two thousand pairs of shoes. Quick, call Imelda. I'd say Finale is definitely worth a visit when you're in the Bay area.

So there you are. If I haven't listed your favorite department store here, call them and ask the operator where their clearance centers are. If she doesn't know check with someone in the executive offices. It could be you have one of these gold mines near you. Oh, I already checked with Bloomingdale's—they just closed their outlet center. A pity.

### *Bottom-of-the-line Chains*

Lowbrow shopping haunts like Kmart, Target (pronouced *tar-jay* by fashion cognoscenti), Sears, JCPenney, and Byrons in Florida, are also worth a visit these days—and not just for tires and Windex, although those items are still readily available. Some of these stores have somehow managed to see beyond their polyester floral shirtwaists and are consciously changing their image. They're now offering up some rather fashionable merchandise—and good value too. The winners are, for the most part, still mixed in with the mundane, but they're easy enough to spot. What to look for? Casual stuff like cotton T-shirts, tanks, camisoles, leggings, shorts, jeans, basic mini-skirts, socks, sweats, cotton sweaters, and the like. Please don't get near those polyester blazers, or the poly stretch pants either for that matter. Also check clothes for kids and teenagers here.

### *Mid-range Discounters*

In between Loehmann's and Target there are a few mid-range discounters worth mentioning. T. J. Maxx (four hundred plus stores nationwide) is one of the best. They carry labels like Calvin Klein and DKNY, and you can sometimes find real bagains like $300 washed-silk jackets reduced by half. Shoes, too, are often a good deal. A friend of mine found a great pair of $125 Joan & David tan sandals there for only $35. The best designer merchandise, though, sells fast, so your timing has to be right-on to score big.

Marshall's (about four hundred stores across the country) carries some designer labels, but not necessarily their top-of-the-line stuff, so it's hit or miss in that department. They are, though, apparently a good source for shoes, and I personally have found some super deals in the men's department: a great soft denim jacket for me ($40, lined), and a Perry Ellis American denim shirt for my husband at half the retail price.

I like Ross Dress for Less (approximately 220 stores, mostly in the South and Southwest) for casual stuff. It's *not* the place to look for chic or elegance. I've gotten great deals on men's sweats ($12 for top quality), plaid flannel shirts ($6, end of the season sale), ladies shorts ($12), tank-type tops (Esprit, $12), even underwear (Cacharel bikinis, $2, Victoria's Secret bikinis, $3). But there's a lot of middle-of-the-road merchandise to sort through, so it takes patience. A finely tuned eye is also a big help.

There are also smaller regional chains that could be worth checking out if you live in the area. Daffy's, for instance, (ten stores in New York, New Jersey, Virginia, and Philadelphia) is reputed to carry some of the better designers. Annie Sez, (fifty-one stores up and down the eastern seaboard) is supposedly in the same stylistic ballpark, and then there's Mandee's, (134 stores—also on eastern seaboard), which reportedly specializes in more junior-sized merchandise. Since off-price stores are becoming more and more popular, I can only assume there are a bunch more that I haven't even heard of. Listen to your local grapevine for news of good shops with good deals.

## Catalogs

Catalogs can be a blessing for busy women with no time to shop. The risks? Not too many really if you order from a reliable firm. If an item doesn't meet with your full approval you can just call UPS and send it back. The only snag is that most of the time you pay return shipping costs. You pay the original shipping cost as well, so if an item turns out to be a total bust, you're out about $10. But you've saved on gas and time shopping. So maybe it all evens out.

Catalogs, through, are best for basics, simple designs, and casual attire. Ordering cocktail dresses, silk suits, etc., is definitely trickier, since fit is more crucial and fabric and drape are so important.

And . . .

- If you're uncertain about sizing ask the order clerk for his or her suggestion. Take the advice and ask if the company will pay for the return if it doesn't work out. Some will comply.
- Loose, roomy sweaters, cotton turtlenecks, pajama tops, and the like are obviously surer fit bets than pants and fitted jackets. Shoes are always questionable.
- Beware of catalogs that seem to be offering too good a deal. I once ordered a pair of fine-looking moccasin slippers from a cheapo catalog that were advertised for $6.95. They were hardly worth that. They were paper thin and very poorly made. On the other hand I bought my husband a pair of slipper moccasins for $30 something from Lands' End that were better than anything I've yet to see in the stores.
- If you decide to go the catalog route get to know your catalogs as well as you know your stores. Their quality and sizing is generally consistent. Once you know how their medium size T-shirts fit you, for instance, you can call and ask if the knit shirt you're interested in is as roomy or less roomy than the T. Same goes for fabric weight. "Is it the same quality cotton as the #2490 shirt I ordered last month?" you could ask.
- Pricey store catalogs like Saks and Neiman-Marcus are fun to look at but no great shakes bargainwise. I personally wouldn't bother.

• Don't order items that you could easily get on sale at your neighborhood mall. There's no sense in ordering a pair of Keds for $26.99 (including shipping) when they normally sell for $22 in a department store and can be found on sale for $16.

Although I get most of the best catalogs, I very seldom order merchandise. I personally like to feel a fabric and see the drape of a garment before I buy, and after all these years, I have to admit I still like the thrill of finding a bargain. I do, on the other hand, have some very fashion-savvy friends who shop catalogs all the time and swear by them.

The following are their favorites—plus a few selected comments and advice.

(NOTE: Most of these catalogs have 800 numbers, so if they sound interesting to you, give them a call and ask them to send you their latest edition. Catalogs are free, so you really can't go wrong. Even if you don't order anything you might get some ideas.)

J. Crew, 1 Ivy Crescent, Lynchburg, VA 24513-1001
(1-800-562-0258, twenty-four hours, seven days a week).
Everybody's favorite, great basics. Reasonable prices.

Tweeds, 1 Avery Row, Roanoke, VA 24012-8528
(customer service: 1-800-444-9449, 9 A.M. to 9 P.M. Monday to Friday).
Number two favorite. Very wearable stuff.

Victoria's Secret, 3425 Stelzer, Columbus, OH 43069 (1-800-888-8200, twenty-four hours, seven days a week).
Great underwear of course, but also some surprisingly tempting clothes.

Clifford & Wills, 1 Clifford Way, Asheville, NC 28810
(1-800-922-1035, twenty-four hours, seven days a week).

Smith & Hawken Clothing, 25 Corte Madera, Mill Valley, CA 94941-1829 (415-383-2000, 5 A.M. to 9 P.M. Monday to Friday, 7 A.M. to 6 P.M. Saturday, 8 A.M. to 5 P.M. Sunday).

Lands' End, 1 Lands' End Lane, Dodgeville, WI 53595
(1-800-356-4444, twenty-four hours, seven days a week).

The J. Peterman Company, 2444 Palumbo Drive, Lexington, KY 40509-1102 (1-800-231-7341, 8 A.M. to 10 P.M., seven days a week).

Patagonia, P.O. Box 8900, Bozeman, MT 59795
(1-800-638-6464 for orders, 7 A.M. to 7 P.M. weekdays, 9 to 5 Saturday;
1-800-523-9597 for questions, Monday to Friday 8 to 4:30).
Great sports and outdoor clothing.

Eddie Bauer, P.O. Box 3700, Seattle, WA 98124 (1-800-426-8020,
4 A.M. to 11 P.M., seven days a week). Good for outdoor clothing. Basics
are very basic.

L. L. Bean, Double L Street, Freeport, ME 04033
(1-800-221-4221, twenty-four hours, 365 days a year). Great active outdoor clothing, etc.

If, after all, you decide that catalogs are more of a bother than a boon,
you can have your name removed from their mailing lists as your personal
contribution to helping the environment. According to EPA reports, direct
mail is responsible for 2.4 percent of the nation's municipal solid waste.

There are a few ways to go:

1. The all-or-nothing approach is to write to the Mail Preference Service
department of the Direct Marketing Association, 11 West 42 Street, P.O.
Box 3861, New York, NY, 10163-3861. They will delete your name, free of
charge, from most national lists. This will, within four months, terminate
almost *all* of your direct mail, including your one favorite catalog. So think
twice on this one.

2. To keep your favorite catalogs coming but to reduce other direct mail
marketing solicitations, alert your catalog company that you want your name
eliminated from the customer lists that they sell to other firms (a standard
practice). Most of the catalogs listed above have a mail list option paragraph
on their order form that tells you how to do it. Usually they ask that you
send your catalog mailing label with a note asking that your name not be
sold.

3. To cancel specific catalogs send the individual companies a postcard
requesting your name be taken off their mailing list. Even that will help cut
down the clutter at your local landfill.

## *Miscellaneous Shopping Places*
*Vintage clothing shows* are a great source. You can almost always find a few
unique pieces of clothing and/or accessories that can be blended with your
basics to add real individual panache. Antique stores find a lot of their
merchandise at these shows, then generally give them a hearty markup

before passing them on to the consumer. You can save a bundle by buying directly from the shows and cutting out the middleman. Major vintage shows are held annually (sometimes more often) in New York, California, Seattle, Indianapolis, Connecticut, Massachusetts, and Toronto. Schedules and information for most of the various shows are listed in *The Vintage Gazette,* a quarterly eight-page newsletter, published by vintage textile and clothing mavin, Molly Turner. Subscriptions cost $10.00 per year or $15.00 for two years, but Molly says she'd also be happy to send you a one-time sample for $2.00. Write to *The Vintage Gazette,* 194 Amity Street, Amherst, MA 01002, or call Molly direct at 413-549-6446.

*Auctions* used to yield some terrific deals, but unfortunately the big ones like Sotheby's and Christie's no longer hold clothing auctions in the States. According to Sotheby's it's simply no longer economical. If you like the idea of auctions, though, you might want to do a little research and find out if the better auction houses in your area hold old clothing auctions—or if they ever include clothing in their estate sales. You could get lucky and find a beaded or velvet jacket, a beaded bag, or a great coat or gown by Chanel, Mainbocher, Fortuny, or Balenciaga. But these days, I'm afraid, auctions, when you can find them, are more of a pleasant diversion than a wearable clothing source.

On the complete opposite end of the fashion spectrum are the great, often cheap, fun finds that can be found off the beaten path in unexpected places. Examples: army-navy stores for old bomber jackets, western stores for cowboy boots, hats and belts; sports stores for rugby shirts and weight-lifting belts; five and tens for cheap canvas shoes; ethnic communities for Ukrainian amber jewelry, Indian kurtas, African mud cloth and Berber hand-stitched leather shoes, Guatemalan vests, Chinese shoes, quilted jackets, kung fu jackets, Japanese kimonos, zori, hapi coats, obis, and Mexican silver jewelry and embroidered cottons. The point is not to limit yourself to the malls. America's melting pot is cooking, and we might as well take advantage of it—and learn a little about our new citizens as well.

If you're ever in Los Angeles and have a few hours to kill, stroll along the Venice boardwalk. You can always find great deals, especially great cheap jewelry and designer clone sunglasses. Glasses go for approximately $7.00 —UV coating and everything. And as an extraspecial bonus you'll probably get to rub elbows (or biceps) with a few hulking bodybuilders.

## HOME SEWING

Just a quick word on home sewing: If you own a sewing machine and you have any extra time at all—think about it. You can save an enormous amount of money, and you don't have to be a genius seamstress to whip up a few simple basics for yourself. There are plenty of easy-to-sew styles that require no more than a few well-placed seams.

The biggest plus of home sewing is the freedom of fabric choice it allows. When you buy ready-to-wear clothing your material choices are relatively limited, which is why shopping usually takes so much time. You might find a garment with the exact design and fit you were looking for, but in the wrong color and texture fabric. When you make your own clothes you pick the design *and* the material. You can also turn very simple styles into sophisticated designs by clever contrasting of fabrics. You could, for instance, line a striped cardigan with a small polka-dot pattern, or use a small black-and-white checked material on the inside of a black blouse collar.

The pattern companies have designs for every level of sewing expertise: very easy for novices (simple little tops for under jackets, straight short skirts) to designer haute couture lines for seasoned professionals. If you're interested but don't know where to start, pick up one of the introductory sewing guides put out by the pattern companies and give it a try. Even if it turns out that sewing clothing isn't your thing, you could always turn out a set of curtains or a few pillows while the dust is off the machine.

Also think accessories. When you go through the stores always watch for fun little accessories that can be easily duplicated with a quick turn of a needle—for one fourth the price. Our old friend Ronnie has been known to sew trimming lace on men's square cotton handkerchiefs to wear in her blazer pocket. She's also sewn little pearls on lace doilies (another pocket stuffer), and even stitched sequins and beads all over a bustier, which she said looked sensational but was a little tough on her fingers. Imagination is the name of the game. And time? If you have enough time to sit and watch *Murphy Brown* you have enough time to sew on a few metaphorical pearls.

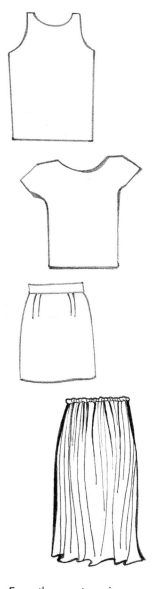

Even the most novice seamstress can whip together designs like these.

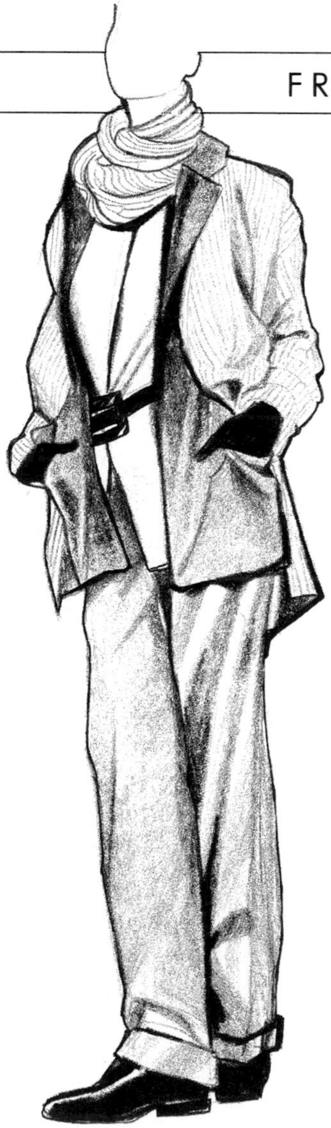

FROM BASICS TO SPECIAL OCCASIONS,

# CHAPTER 8

# *The Nineties' Wardrobe*

## INCLUDING TV WEAR AND PREGNANCY

I n the nineties wardrobes can pretty much be broken down into traditional career clothes, weekend casuals, and special event attire. By traditional careers I mean those that have a somewhat formal or conservative
air about them, such as banking, law, politics, etc. In less formal working
arenas you can usually go for the high end of weekend casuals—that is, Gap
plus.

Unfortunately I'm not personally there with each of you to discuss the
various aspects of your life-styles and figures, so I have to count on you to
interpret the suggestions in this chapter to fit your *individual* needs. If I
propose loose baggy trousers, for instance, and you know from your newly
culled expertise that they are totally wrong for your body type, simply substitute pencil-slim pants or even a long skirt to get the look that's right for you.
If I say tank top and you'd be better in a V neck, substitute. Same goes for
quantity. I'll be talking here about *minimum* pared-down wardrobe require-
ments. If your individual life-style calls for additions and your pocketbook
allows it, you have my blessings to buy more and personally help move the
economy along.

First, a few reminders:

- You don't have to change your *entire* wardrobe every day. So buy the
  best and buy less. You're better off wearing a few quality garments
  than a slew of mediocre ones. You won't need as many clothes and
  your life will be simpler.

- Buy clothing that requires minimum fidgeting and readjusting. You should be able to put something on in the morning and forget about it until you take it off at night. That is true nineties' comfort.
- Think classics that can be easily layered and dressed up or down with accessories.
- Plan your wardrobe around a base neutral color and supplementary colors that all mix and match. Color matches today are more forgiving than in the past. Colors simply have to harmonize or coordinate rather than match exactly. Even an old taboo like mixing pure whites with other like shades such as cream, ivory, or ecru is perfectly acceptable today. In fact, it looks fabulous.
- Find your style uniform. The more consistent you are with your basic style, the fewer shoes, bags, and miscellaneous accessories you'll need. If your casual uniform silhouette is slim pants and cardigans, for instance, you wouldn't need many more shoes than a pair of Keds, sandals, and/or flat ballet slippers.

Essentially we all need clothes for work, play, at home, and special occasions. *The biggest part of your wardrobe should be devoted to the area in which you spend the most time.* If you go to work in a traditional corporate environment five days a week, you'll obviously need more silk shirts and panty hose than someone who sits at home and writes all day. So I'll leave it up to you to decide exactly how many you need of these nineties' wardrobe basics.

## THE BASICS

### A SUIT

Everybody needs a great suit. Not the old kind of going-to-church suit or the straight-jacketed, John Malloy dress-for-success suit of the seventies, but the *new* suit: a comfortable, easy-to-wear jacket matched up with great slouchy trousers or a shortish skirt that can look intimidatingly corporate, gamin and boyish, or downright glamorous, depending on how you wear it.

The new suit is one of the nineties' handiest fashion staples since it's equally at home with a camisole, a T-shirt, a fabulous silk blouse, or—why not—even a bustier. It can be made of heavy washed silk, lightweight wool gabardine, wool crepe, or even a good quality rayon. The pieces should be ultimately adaptable: a jacket design that's totally compatible with the style and mood of your general wardrobe (see Chapter 4) and that can be worn with anything from jeans to dresses, a skirt that can perhaps be worn with an overblouse or cardigan, and/or trousers that are comfy enough for a

The four-piece suit: jacket, trousers, and two skirts of different lengths.

Different looks for different moods utilizing the four-piece suit and a few nineties' wardrobe basics.

casual weekend movie date. A four-piece suit would really be ideal (if it's compatible with your body type): a jacket, a conservative business-length skirt, a short skirt, and trousers. Then you'd really be set for almost all occasions.

Although it would be heaven to have an Armani or two in your closet, your suit doesn't have to be precoordinated by a designer. If you're on an extremely tight budget you might find it cheaper to put together a suit yourself. What's the difference between a suit and a jacket cum skirt or slacks anyway? In a "real" suit the pieces match, that's all. They're the same fabric and sold together as a unit. Well, there's no reason you can't put together pieces yourself. Find a jacket you love and track down a great pair of slacks and a skirt or two that match.

Fabrics don't have to match exactly, they just have to come close. If you stick to the basic color strategy described in Chapter 3 and buy your wardrobe basics (slacks, jackets, cardigans, and skirts) in your favorite base neutral color, your "suit" will automatically evolve as you shop.

Black is by far the easiest neutral for the do-it-yourself suit scheme, since it's a cinch to match pieces (and black glides so effortlessly into evening). The more esoteric your base neutral color, the harder it is to find suitable matches. You might have to start with a real suit.

If you dress mostly in ultra-casual Gap-type clothes, the new four-piece suit is just about the only "real clothes" you'll need, except maybe a basic black dress. You could wear the suit to a tony restaurant (the mini with a camisole), a serious business meeting, or a media interview (the regulation-length skirt with a silk shirt), a comedy club (the slacks, T-shirt, and sneaks), or even a wedding (add pearls). Plus, of course, you can wear the jacket with your jeans.

Since a suit (or the separate suit pieces) will comprise your most important wardrobe foundation pieces, buy quality and buy carefully. You should *definitely* try on a few Donna Karans, Armanis, Calvin Kleins, Ralph Laurens, or the like first to get a feel for contemporary classic simplicity. You want these garments to last.

### A FEW OTHER JACKETS

Aside from your basic suit jacket you will probably want a few others, perhaps one in white linen or raw silk for summer, a denim type for hanging out, and a wool tweed or navy blazer for winter and fall. Jackets are great for work and play and are an extremely important part of a successful nineties' wardrobe. (See the jacket section in Chapter 5.)

### A COUPLE OF CARDIGANS (PREFERABLY CASHMERE)

Cardigans are sweaters that are open at the front like a jacket. They're great toppers and make for a nice casual layered look. They're especially handy for lazing around inside when a jacket might feel like too much, and also perfect in most office environments. Aside from their classic wool incarnations you can also find them around in Gap-type cottons for casual summer wear. (Any of you into *totally* irrelevant fashion trivia should know that these fine wardrobe staples were named for the Earl of Cardigan who apparently sported one during the Crimean War—1855.)

### A ''LITTLE BLACK DRESS'' IN SILK

This is your special occasion uniform when any of the suit variations won't work. If black is not your color, choose another dark neutral like midnight blue. Separates that look like a dress are just fine.

### A FEW SILK BLOUSES

Try to get one light and one dark that blend beautifully with your base neutral color. They should be of exquisite design and quality, and stylishly complement your suit.

### A COUPLE OF FINE-QUALITY COTTON SHIRTS

One white, the other your choice.

### THREE PAIRS OF TROUSERS

Aside from the trousers from your four-piece suit you'll need a pair of black tailored wool slacks (if your suit is black get a pair of classic gray flannels) for winter, a light linen and/or raw silk for summer, and a pair of black silk pants. Styles should go with jackets and be able to be upgraded with a silk blouse or casualized with a T-shirt. If you are not a trouser person substitute skirts here.

## TWO SKIRTS

One in your base neutral color in a summer fabric, the other in the same color in a wool gabardine. The styles should be figure flattering and proportionally in sync with your jackets.

## A COUPLE OF GOOD WOOL OR COTTON PULLOVERS

## A SMASHING OVERCOAT

This is a prime investment so think longevity. The line should be simple and flattering, fabric should be first-class, workmanship should be high caliber, and color should be a versatile neutral that doesn't show dirt easily. Bright colors like red can definitely lend cheer to a blustery winter day, but would not cross over into evening as easily as a dark neutral. Black, charcoal, or navy cashmere would be smart choices.

Check designer discount stores before paying anywhere near full price. (See previous chapter.) Two years ago I bought a fabulous classic black Perry Ellis coat in a soft cashmere/wool blend at Loehmann's for around $300.00. It's perfect for night and day and I plan to wear it well through this decade. It would have cost twice as much at regular retail. So shop around.

## A PAIR OR TWO OF JEANS OR KHAKIS

In jeans go for simple, basic, no-frills American style with no trendy detailing like sewn-in belts or front panels. All jeans fit differently so be prepared to try on a bunch till you find your brand. Wrangler and Lee seem to be the cheapest. Levi's 560, Gap Classics, and Armani A/X Classic (the costliest) have gotten the best reviews for fit and style.

## THREE OR FOUR CAMISOLES OR TANK TOPS

Choose the type that can stand on their own or be worn under things. (At least one should be silk.)

## A SMALL COLLECTION OF COTTON T-SHIRTS (MORE THAN A FEW IN WHITE)

You'll *definitely* need a bunch of these prima nineties' staples. Wear them alone, under jackets, under V-necked sweaters, under cowl necks. For color, for warmth . . . they are indispensable. Line up your T-shirt sources. Try men's departments or JCPenney–type chain stores where they are usu-

A super gala uniform. Black silk basics topped with some kind of beaded jacket or an evening coat like this will be appropriate and smashing right into the next century.

ally cheaper. Good T-shirts are a heavier gauge cotton and usually shrink, so buy a larger size to start. Don't forget to buy a few V necks for summer.

*Great tip:* When wearing regular crewneck T-shirts under sweaters or shirts or with jackets, try wearing them backwards for a better neckline. Most T-shirts, especially large ones, slip too low in the front. When worn backwards they have a straighter, higher, neck. If T-shirts are too thin try wearing two together.

Essentially that's the way a modern wardrobe framework should look. Any other noninvestment additions are totally optional and individual. Add as many as you like: cotton turtlenecks, leggings, summer shorts, little cotton skirts, sweats, etc. With clever shopping you should be able to find any of the above for between $5 and $20 apiece. (See previous chapter.)

One or two pairs of pumps, a pair of loafers, a pair of boots, a pair of sandals, and a pair or two of sneakers, loafers or moccasins should do the trick. It's not much—but that's the point—you truly don't need much.

## SPECIAL OCCASIONS

### Galas

Within the preceding general framework, you'll find yourself set for almost any situation, with the exception of bona fide black-tie affairs. You've got a few ways to go here—borrow from a friend, rent, or be prepared yourself. Whenever possible, I recommend the latter.

The main thing is not to panic when the invitation arrives or be cowed by the grandiosity of an event. You don't need to make your entrance in piles of baubles, ruffles, and taffeta no matter how high-toned the occasion. Simplicity is still the name of the game. You are much better off forgetting the fancy, fussy frills and making your statement with a sleek, simple understated design in a brilliant fabric. Silks, satins, panne velvet, subtle metallics, or sequins will immediately set an august tone. Bottom line: Again think Audrey Hepburn—if she wouldn't have worn it, you shouldn't either.

Since budget is still one of our major concerns, black is once again your wisest color choice. The first time you wear a red evening dress it can look lovely, the second it will look familiar, the third time it will look old. Black, on the other hand, is so much less obvious that you could wear the same tasteful ensemble to posh events for years without causing a single raised eyebrow. Black is always perfectly suitable and elegant, provides the sleekest of evening silhouettes, and can easily accommodate a switch of accessories for occasional updates. You can get so much more mileage out of black evening clothes that it's hardly worth considering another color. Yes, it's true that Audrey Hepburn *did* wear a *red* one-shouldered gown to the 1991 Academy Awards, but Audrey was not cost conscious—she was merely elegant. She always knew she could pick up a new Givenchy when she needed one.

The most practical design approach is to build the total look with pieces that are simple in shape but luxurious in texture. A long narrowish black silk charmeuse skirt, for instance, paired with a softly draped sequined tunic, a simple dolman-sleeved deep V-necked charmeuse blouse, or even a charmeuse camisole and quilted silk jacket would be perfectly lovely. The tops could also be paired with soft, silk trousers or even a silk miniskirt for completely different silhouettes. Separates, even in evening wear, are a lot more versatile than a dress or gown that only has one look. When money is an issue, versatility is always key.

Whenever you're in the stores keep your eyes open for pieces with "formal potential." After-Christmas sales are a particularly good time to pick up black silks, sequins, and dressy holiday metallics.

## TV Interviews

Another special occasion I want to touch on very briefly is the television interview—since we are, after all, in the Media Age. Andy Warhol once said that we will all have our fifteen minutes of fame, and yours could be rapidly approaching. If you are an expert in any given field, a mover and shaker in your community, or have ever dated a recovering alcoholic co-dependent who is also the son of a cross dressing ex-Mafia don, there's a chance that you could be booked by Phil, Oprah, Geraldo, or maybe Maury. At the very least you could have thirty seconds on the local news.

So a few tips on what to wear on camera:

- Keep it simple. No plaids, busy prints, stripes, or polka dots. If you follow the *Dress Like a Million* plan you won't have many anyway.
- Wear your most flattering secondary color or a combination of your base neutral with a bright. Bold, solid colors look very nice. Off-white works better than stark white. Black by itself will drain the color from your face and make you look older, which—just a guess—you'd probably rather not. Exception: black beading, sequins, satins, and other dressy fabrics can look quite wonderful because they reflect the light rather than absorb it—something to keep in mind for your Oscar acceptance speech.
- Wear a top with a simple flattering neckline. If you say anything remotely emotional they will zip in for a close-up. Most of the time

you will be cropped somewhere between your waist and mid-bust . . . unless you wear a miniskirt.

- So don't wear a miniskirt. If they seat you on a high stool or one of their standard uncomfortable chairs it can prove quite awkward.
- It's usually a good idea to wear some sort of jacket or cardigan affair to which they can easily attach their little microphone. If you don't—say you have on a simple silk shell—they will either try to punch a hole in it, scrunch it up and clip it, or if they have the time, have you run a wire up under the blouse. All in all it's easier to wear something that's easy to clip on to.
- If you expect to be in the studio and on camera for more than five minutes wear a T-shirt under any silks—and bring an extra sweater or even a blanket. They will want you there way before you have to be and you will have to wait in some freezing room. Then when you get on camera and under the lights you may perspire. The T-shirt will absorb perspiration before it stains your silks. The extra sweater and/ or blanket will keep you cozy beforehand and offer security. Break a leg. . . .

## PREGNANCY

Pregnancy is a special occasion that will have a much longer lasting effect on your life than your television interview. First off, consider yourself lucky that you are pregnant at a time when its easier than ever to find suitable clothing. There are so many big tops, leggings, baggy pants, and roomy jackets around these days that you may never have to set foot into an official maternity store, and if you do, you're bound to find a lot more simple shifts, denim jumpers, and no-nonsense business outfits than in days of yore.

The most important thing to keep in mind is that your basic style doesn't have to change just because you're in a family way. If you've always been a tailored, tweedy type or a jeans and sneakers person, stay that way. Pregnancy causes all sorts of hormonal changes, but as far as we know there are none that are directly linked to, or result in, a sudden and frenzied craving for pastels, polyester, and bows. Keep your identity. Simply make some minor style revisions to accommodate your changing body shape.

Between you and your husband you probably already own plenty of clothing that can double as maternity wear:

- all your big tops, overblouses, roomy sweaters
- any of your husbands sweaters, shirts, T-shirts, sweats, and jackets that he's willing to share (don't forget to roll up the sleeves)

- most pants with drawstrings or elastic waistbands
- leggings
- leotards and expandable Lycra body suits
- wrap skirts and cotton skirts with elastic waistbands.

If you have a very casual life-style, you may not need much more than that, since you can probably get by with your regular clothes for your first trimester. If you're a traditional working woman, however, you'll probably have to do some shopping, so keep the following in mind:

- Your maternity wardrobe should be just as mix and matchable as your regular wardrobe. In fact, maybe even more so, since it will be even more compact and pared down.
- Try buying standard items a couple of sizes larger than usual. And think about designs that can also be worn stylishly in the transition time *after* you give birth but before you get back to your fighting weight.
- Your best colors are still your best colors, but you might want to concentrate on the darker shades, since they're not only the most slimming but show less wear and tear. Wear light colors, if you like, near your face to draw attention up and away from your tummy. Unless you're model tall, your best bet will be monochromatic outfits. If top and bottom colors are too different you will look shorter and wider.
- For nice big tops check big women stores like Lane Bryant.
- Almost any old skirt can be easily converted into maternity wear. Simply have your friendly tailor sew in an expandable stretch panel around the top. Afterwards you can still wear the skirt under big sweaters and tops.
- Some pants and even jeans can be likewise converted.
- Tapered pants will probably be more flattering than full baggy ones, since they'll accentuate one of the few areas where you haven't gained weight.
- Capes, shawls, and ponchos are great cover-ups that you will never outgrow. Also pick up an inexpensive lightweight waterproof poncho at a camping or sporting goods store for those unexpected showers.
- Kimono-style jackets are wonderfully stylish, comfortable, and so size versatile they can be worn before, during, and after your pregnancy. It might be the one garment you might think about having made, perhaps in a dark shade of cashmere or fine cotton knit. It could be part of your pregnancy uniform.

- Since your body temperature tends to go up when you're pregnant cottons are your best bet. Heavy wools, tweeds, and the like will not be very comfortable. Nor will pure synthetics—you're breathing for two now.

- If the elastic gets too tight on the waist of any elastic-banded shorts, pants, sweats, or skirts, check to see if you can replace it yourself with a longer piece. Open the inside seam a tad at the waist, catch the elastic with a tweezer, and give it a tug. If it comes out easily remove it. Then buy some new elastic at a fabric or notion store, attach a nice long piece to a small safety pin and slip the pin with elastic attached through the opening where you took the old piece out. Work it through the waistband, and when it comes out the other side adjust to size and either knot or sew the two pieces together.

- If pants or skirts are starting to feel too binding as you come to term, try oversized men's overalls on weekends and after hours, perhaps over fun plaid shirts. Wear jumpers for workdays.

- If you need to have nonmaternity dresses hemmed have them made a little longer in the front than the back to accommodate baby growth.

- Find sensibly low-heeled shoes. High heels are uncomfortable and unhealthy when you're carrying extra weight. You might need about a half size larger as well. Espadrilles would be a best bet, since they're inexpensive and come in great colors.

- If your pregnancy takes you into the hot summer months you absolutely need to know about lungis (aka sarongs, aka pareos, etc.). They are fabulous as beach cover-ups or for just hanging out in hot weather. Lungis are the everyday fashion staple in much of southeast Asia, and since they are wrapped, not sewn, they are ultimately adjustable and wonderfully comfortable. A lungi (as they are called in Myanmar) is essentially a rectangular piece of cloth, usually a lovely ethnic floral with a border, sometimes a hand-dyed batik, that is approximately $3\frac{1}{2}$ feet by 6 feet, and is wrapped around the waist as a skirt or above the breasts as a sort of shift. In Asia subtle nuances in wrapping techniques indicate the origin and often the gender of the wrapee. In Myanmar, for instance, the cloth is first sewn together at the ends forming a wide tube and then wrapped on the side for women, and in the center for men. Most everyplace else they wrap and tie without being sewn into a tube.

    If you have any friends heading to anywhere in Asia ask them to bring you back a few. Prices range from around $7 to as much as $50 (for the artistic hand-printed or silk-screen variety), and they're relatively easy to find. In places like Bali they're even sold at the duty-

free airport stores (although at a considerably higher price than in local native shops). If you can't come by a real one, simply buy a lovely piece of fabric and make your own. See the illustrations above for the most common wrapping technique, then play around and invent a few wraps yourself.

Needless to say, if you're approaching pregnancy for the first time, it pays to chat with all your fashion-savvy friends who have already been through it. They're bound to have even more tips, hints, and ideas.

Here's one personal viewpoint from my friend, actress Erin Grey, who just remarried and gave birth to an adorable little girl.

I didn't have a budget. I was facing bankruptcy [the results of an unpleasant painful divorce from husband number one, don't ask] and was not about to spend money on clothes. It seemed real important for me to use whatever I had in my closet. I only invested in a few things. The first was five midcalf, flowery, antique rayon dresses, that are

Wrapping a lungi is a piece of cake. Hold the fabric behind you at waist level, leaving one side longer than the other. Fold the short side across your front. Wind the top of the long side a bit, then pull the short side snug. Pull the longer, twisted side around your waist and tuck the top of the short side over the twisted part.

sort of flowy, and have little clips in the back so you can let them out or take them in. I bought them my third month, and they were pretty much my staple throughout the pregnancy. They worked for night and day depending on how I dressed them up. I wore them with Keds and little socks during the day, and with silver jewelry and patent leather flats at night. . . . I always wore them very loose, since I couldn't bear to have anything touching my waist. For some reason anything even brushing my waist was just painful and uncomfortable. So these little summer dresses were fabulous—nothing binding on my waistline—they became my little uniform.

The other main thing I invested in were four cotton spandex unitards in extra large—two white and two black. I bought them for $12 each at Doughboys, which is an outlet for irregular blue jeans or something like that. They were like a leotard or body suit with leggings. What's neat is that they were all in one, and offered plenty of support. They were really comfortable. My whole back and belly felt totally supported. . . . Then I'd wear my husband's extra-large T-shirts over them. They were the best thing I invested in.

If I wanted to dress up I'd wear a black unitard under one of my husband's extralarge silk shirts. It looked fabulous. . . . Luckily my husband's six feet four inches so I had a lot of big shirts around to choose from. I'd occasionally wear one of his sweaters or sweatshirts. If you don't have a husband who's extra large . . . this plan may not work out. (She laughs.)

I also bought one blazer—extra large—in the men's department—really nice. I wore it whenever I needed an extra layer. I actually only went to a maternity shop once when I wanted something special for my baby shower. And I did borrow a dress from a girlfriend—a great navy blue pregnancy dress that I wore with a white T-shirt and white Keds—and it was fabulous.

Erin also stresses the importance of setting up support systems—not just for borrowing and exchanging maternity clothes, but to pass along baby clothes after the happy little bundle arrives. "Friends are the best," she says. "There are about four or five of us now who had our babies three and four months apart, so we just keep the baby clothes moving around. We mark our initials on them with a permanent marker so we know who belongs to what because in the end we want the clothes back. But babies only wear one size for about a month so you don't use them that much. We all agreed to use bibs so we make sure the formula gets out of them. . . . It's working out great."

Erin's suggestions for the working woman: "It's tougher, but I think I'd invest in five or so dresses like I did, but probably less floral and more solid colors than I picked. Then I'd tie the look together with a few large blazers and black flats. And I definitely wouldn't hesitate to call up my girlfriends to borrow their maternity clothes. You just have to promise to take good care of them. . . . It's much easier—cheaper too."

## Travel

Your travel wardrobe is simply a microcosm of your already pared-down nineties' wardrobe: a finely-tuned color scheme, versatile comfortable clothing that can be worn a multitude of ways, and a few accessories to add zip and panache.

The quality of your travel wardrobe depends on your purpose, destination, and style of travel, and all three quantifiers should be factored in. Example: Business trips call for chic, quality fashions that present a good successful impression. Business trips to Rio, where petty theft is second only to soccer as a national sport, calls for chic, quality facsimiles for business and poverty chic for sight-seeing. So do a little advance research on where you're going.

Duration of stay is another consideration—but less of one than you might think. The bottom line: If it will do you for a week, it will do you for a month. If you need an extra shirt, they are sold all over the world. Travel light, it's more fun. All you really need for pure pleasure travel is something that is more or less appropriate for most situations. You do not need the perfect red belt or the perfect pair of heels. You can be less picky on the road. Ideally everything should be able to fit in one easily carried bag that can slide under the airplane seat.

Margo Werts travels back and forth to Europe about six times a year for business and pleasure, and has her travel wardrobe down to a fine science. "Black, almost everything is black," she says. "I have black leggings, big black cashmere turtleneck sweater, black flat shoes, and a black evening coat for night, that goes with a little skirt so it's kind of elegant. Then I have a pair of little glittery hoops [earrings] . . . and that's it for evening. For day I bring a gray men's suit—high waisted, pleated pants with a gray blazer and a few vests. I pack an extra black turtleneck and black ski pants, and that's it. I'm ready to go. Oh, and a man's overcoat."

The great thing about packing for a trip after being on the *Dress Like a Million* system for a while is that so much of your wardrobe already works together—both colorwise and proportionately—that the challenge is never finding the right things to pack, but rather making yourself leave certain things behind—because everything is *just* right. In the long run that's a much easier route to go.

# CHAPTER 9

# *Topping It All Off*

## HAIR, MAKEUP, AND A FIT BODY

While your clothes do a hefty percent of the work in creating your image, your hair, makeup, carriage, and grooming, have an enormous effect on your total presentation, so they deserve some serious attention here. If you've already got all these elements under control, you probably don't need my help, but if you have even a modicum of suspicion that any of them are working against you rather than for you, read on.

### HAIR

Let's talk hair first. There's no question that the right hairstyle makes all the difference in the world. Your hair is your ultimate accessory and it should suit you perfectly. So your first step: Line up the best hairdresser in your area—someone who is not only a brilliant cutter, but who has supreme taste and can help you realize your full potential. Even if you can't afford the best for each individual trim, it would behoove you to see a maestro for your initial consultation/cut. Then perhaps find someone less costly, maybe even in the same salon, for regular maintenance. Ask around for recommendations. John Sahag, one of New York's top hairstylists, suggests stopping anyone—on the street or wherever—with similarly textured hair (curly, straight, etc.) and a great haircut, and asking her where she gets her hair done. "I don't think it's rude at all," says Sahag. "In fact, it's a compliment. The other woman will love it and be happy to give you the name."

Meanwhile until you find your dream superstylist/consultant here are a few essential tips and hits:

- Realistically assess the quality and texture of your hair. Is it frizzy or straight, fine or lush, curly or wavy? You can't have long, lush intensive curls like Cher when you've got superfine thin hair—unless of course, you can afford one of her wigs. Don't fight it. Figure out what your hair wants to do and then develop a style that incorporates its natural tendencies. Trying to get your hair to lie one way when it grows the other is a constant and frustrating battle.

- Factor in your life-style. *Career*—if you work in any kind of mainstream office you need a hairstyle that allows you to be a worker among workers, not one that screams out for attention or is the antithesis of general office sensibilities. *Play*—if sporting activities are a good part of your life, choose a style that's accommodating. If you swim every day at lunch, for instance, or do a lot of sailing, you do not want some complicated fluffy coif that needs to be thoroughly blow-dried to look good. And consider just how much time and energy you really do want to devote to your hair daily.

- Think low-maintenance. A style that needs professional trimming every two weeks might prove too expensive. (If you wear bangs, have your hairdresser show you how to trim them yourself.) If you have to spend more than twenty minutes on your hair every morning it's time for a new hairdo.

- Your hairstyle should be consistent with your clothing style. Tailored classic clothing calls for a trim classic hairdo. A trendier overall image can handle a trendier do.

- Be aware of the mood and proportion of particular outfits. Padded shoulders, for instance, call for a smaller head. A crewneck sweater, on the other hand, easily accommodates longer tresses. Often just a simple hair comb or barrette will be enough to shift proportion.

- Don't get stuck in an era. Just because your long, straight, glossy, hair won you praise and adoration in the seventies doesn't mean you have to wear it that way for the rest of your life. If you are like the rest of us, your face subtly changes as you age, and your hairdo should follow suit. A style that is flattering on an eighteen-year-old face may only accentuate new lines on a forty-five-year-old face. A case in point is Mary, of Peter, Paul, and Mary fame, who wears her hair now exactly the way she did twenty-five years ago. It looked great then; it looks terrible now. She now needs a style that will help lift her face, not one that drags it down and accentuates wrinkles and extra weight. She also still tries to flip her hair around when she sings, but alas, her hair is too tired and has lost its bounce. The moral: Give some serious thought to the question, Am I wearing my hair this way because it looks good now, or because it looked good then? (If any of you know Crystal Gale, please mention this to her.)

- Use your hairdo to help create the illusions you want. Some styles can make you look taller, shorter, etc. Asymmetrical styles, such as pulling the hair up on one side or cutting one side shorter than the other, for instance, will lead the eye in an upward angle and make you appear taller. Very long hair parted in the center à la 1965 on the other hand, will make you look shorter (and need I say, totally out of it). Short curly hair can add an inch or two, especially if it's cut narrower on the sides. And long hair worn up makes the neck look longer, as do most shorter styles.

- Consider your body type. Head and body shape should be in proportion. Small women look foolish carrying around volumes of hair on their head. Most large women need some hair volume for balance. (See Chapter 2.)

- Consider your face shape and features. Geri Cusenza, the visionary creative director of Sebastian International, says hair can be a terrific corrector. It can slenderize a round face, help balance a square face, widen a too-narrow face, and visually change the proportion of a diamond- or heart-shaped face. It can also make noses look longer or shorter and eyes look bigger. These are the kinds of basics that Geri refers to as "hairdressing 101," and feels all good hairstylists should know.

    Just in case yours doesn't, a few general tips from Geri:

A round face needs a diagonal line, either a bang or a part, or something that keeps it from appearing like a circle.

Short hair is better on smaller faces.

Women with low foreheads *can* wear bangs if they are cut from a triangular part rather than a curved one.

Women with long faces need a layered haircut, since hair all one length drags the face down.

Too much hair covering the face is totally passé and makes you look insecure.

- If you color or highlight your hair, try to stay close to your own natural color. A total turnabout tends to look contrived and calls for expensive wardrobe adjustments. (And never perm and color at the same time.)
- Gray hair makes you look older regardless of age, not that looking older is necessarily negative, but it can be depressing when you're in your thirties and forties. Let's face it, gray hair looks best on women seventy something. If your are in your mid-forties and someone tells you they love your gray hair, examine their motives and have your hair colored that week—by a good colorist, please. Remember, though, skin tends to get lighter as you get older. So if you do opt to cover your gray think about a *slightly* lighter tone than you wore in your heyday.
  NOTE: Color your hair in *natural* shades. Overbleached blonde, screaming red, and poodle black can be effective on rock stars, but is it you?
- For a quick change, there are plenty of styling gels, sprays, creams, and "muds" around that can temporarily change your hair texture—and get it to stay where you want it to stay.

  A few product tips from Ms. Cusenza:

Women with extrafine hair should beware of products with extra hold, since these will only weight their hair down. Instead look for products with light hold.

Switch shampoos at least once a month. Hair gets limp and dull from using the same shampoo too long.

Find a few styling products that work for you. Geri says nobody needs fifty different products in their medicine chests. (And she makes them!)

There are also plenty of what Sahag refers to as "gizmos" on the market—benders, round brushes for blow-drying, different sizes and types of rollers. Sahag's favorite roller is the old-fashioned, quick drying, spring and net curlers (the kind you pin on with bobby pins and used to see covered with a pink cotton hairnet on women in the line at the supermarket checkout). Use the smaller ones for curlier, funkier looks, larger ones for looser curls. Sahag doesn't personally like Velcro rollers. He says they make the ends look like they've "gone through shock treatment." His roller tip of the week: If you don't want your hair to look like it was set, à la the sixties, dampen only the *roots* of the hair section, or just the *length* of the hair section, not both. Apparently this leaves less of a demarcation line and makes for a much more contemporary look.

- For a longer lasting texture change there are always straighteners and perms. Perming techniques have improved a lot over the last few years, making results a lot more predictable and natural looking. Most hairdressers agree that if you can tell it's a perm it's not a good one.

According to experts, the biggest problem with perms is miscommunication. So make it very clear to your hairstylist just *how much* curl you want. Better yet bring in pictures. Your idea of a body wave might be her idea of tight frizz. The larger the perm rod used the larger the curl, so if you ask for a very loose wave and your stylist starts twining your hair around tiny little blue rods tell her to *stop*. Also let her know just how much time you want to spend to get your finished look each day. She should know if you want to wash and run, or if you have the patience to blow-dry. And ask about spot perms that just perm the roots of the hair and add volume.

In my book *Dressing Rich* I mentioned three hairstyles that were the mark of classically elegant rich women. Amazingly enough, ten years later, they still are. Which all goes to prove that elegance is one of fashion's slower movers.

For those of you interested in looking classic and elegant, let me briefly recap these styles for you:

- Medium-long hair worn *away* from the face and clipped back or worn up. It can be pinned up into a classic chignon or French twist, or tucked into a modified Gibson girl knot, as Katharine Hepburn has been doing for the last 100 years. Letting a few perfectly thought-out tendrils "slip" out softens and modernizes the look just enough. Long hair can also be styled into a chic French braid, tied at the nape of the neck in a "status pull" à la George Washington, or pulled up into a classic ponytail for that fresh wholesome look. Although a lot of the top models wear their long tresses loose and rangy, it's not a particularly elegant look. It's fine in the boudoir though.
- "Le Lion", a chin-length (or slightly above or below) coif that is the same length all the way around. This is a most versatile haircut and can be worn straight, with a slight wave, slightly permed, pushed back with a hair band, flipped up or under at the ends, and can even be pulled back to accommodate a chignon or braid hairpiece. It's more Christy Turlington than Cindy Crawford.
- The short layered cut. The layering is very subtle and the cut creates a soft flattering frame for the face. Hair can be layered in various ways to flatter most head shapes and necks. This cut provides a lift to the

face that counters those inevitable lines that seem to appear out of no-
where as we grow older. It's also very easily managed and controlled,
which is probably why Nancy Reagan likes it. Warning: Layered cuts
require a hairstylist with taste and vision. At their worst layered cuts can
look terribly mundane and even matronly. Don't get too poofy. Comb
back rather than forward.

One last word on hair: If money is particulary sparse, but your spirit of
adventure is strong—and your career is not dependent on your looks—
you might want to experiment with an advanced training academy, where
haircuts, perms, and color are very cheap since they are done by trainees—
under supervision, of course. At some places like Sebastian they actually
*pay you.* There are apparently academies in almost every state. Geri Cu-

senza, though, makes a clear distinction between training academies like hers, where pros come to learn about new techniques and products, and local beauty schools where total novices learn the basics. The latter she considers very risky.

Another relatively new development is assistant night at top salons. Again, the less experienced fine-tune their skills on your head under the watchful eye of a top pro. Neither of these routes, of course, is for the faint of heart, but the thing to remember about any haircut—and even color and perms for that matter—is that it's not permanent. You always have a second chance.

If you're interested, check with big companies like Paul Mitchell, Redkin, Vidal Sassoon, and Matrix to see if there's an academy near you, or with your best local salon.

Meanwhile, here are a few best bets in L.A. and New York:

Sebastian International, 6109 De Soto Ave, Woodland Hills, CA (818-999-5112). Workshops and seminars are held regularly. Volunteers are paid $25 to $50 in the form of products, check, or both.

John Sahag Salon, 425 Madison Avenue, New York, NY 10017 (212-750-7772). John has a great reputation for great cuts and styling, and really knows his stuff. Assistant night is Wednesday at 6:00—$15 for cut or perm.

Oribe at Elizabeth Arden, 691 Fifth Avenue, New York, NY 10022 (212-319-3910). Oribe is hot—definitely a big favorite of the fashion magazines. He has assistant classes on Monday nights. Cut is $20. Color or highlights, $30.

Frederic Fekkai Beauty Center at Bergdorf Goodman, 754 Fifth Avenue, New York, NY 10022 (212-753-9500). Fekkai is right up there with Oribe on the popularity scale. Training night is Tuesday (except in June through August). Cut or color is $25.

Louis Licari Color Group, 797 Madison Avenue, New York, NY 10021 (212-517-8084). A very popular colorist with an excellent reputation. Class night is Wednesday. Cut or easy color, $15. Highlights, $26, Perm, $55.

Don't forget to check the address again when and if you call for an appointment. We live in a fast changing world.

## MAKEUP

Just how involved you want to get with makeup is a very personal matter. But the truth is that most of us look better with at least a dab of lipstick and a hint of blush. The bottom line is basically this: The more chic and sophisticated your clothes are, the more polished and finished your makeup should be. It's as simple as that. A freshly scrubbed face is perfect with tennis attire, but a classic Chanel suit calls for at least a light foundation or wisp of powder. And formal evening wear raises the makeup ante to the next stage.

The whole idea of makeup is to enhance your natural beauty: to give your skin a flawless glow, to add dimension to cheekbones, drama and sparkle to your eyes, and to play up your positive features. It should not be used to create an entirely new face, unless you're a geisha and/or preparing for on-camera work. Or have serious Tammy Faye Bakker aspirations.

While I have Tammy in mind, I should mention that one of the biggest mistakes women make with cosmetics is overdoing it: heavy foundation, festive rainbow-hued eyeshadow, contrasting lip liner, raccoonlike eye liner, terminally fuchsia cheeks, and giant fuzzy faux lashes. While I haven't done a formal survey, it seems to me that older women tend to go overboard with foundation, while younger women overload on eye makeup. This would seem to support the theory that a good number of women are mired in the look that was prominent when they came of age and began wearing makeup.

It's important to keep up with the times. Pancake makeup hasn't been hot for a few decades, and Twiggy is an actress now. Today's look, while a step beyond the no-makeup look of the eighties, is still relatively light and natural (like food). Even false eyelashes, which have staged a flash temporary comeback, should look real.

Applying makeup is as individual as your face, and to use makeup to your best advantage it helps to understand all the nuances of your bone structure, coloring, and skin texture. You also should know about all the latest application techniques, products, and other tricks of the trade. If you're less than savvy in these areas think about seeing a professional makeup consultant.

The cheapest consultant, aside from a knowledgeable friend, is the one you find at a department store cosmetics counter demonstrating a particular company's latest line. The makeover is free but the motive is questionable. Generally these experts are more geared to selling products than imparting wisdom. But even so, you may be able to pick up a few pointers—and, as I've noted, the price is certainly right. The trick to reaping rewards from one of these consultations is (1) telling the consultant right off the bat what you're looking for, i.e., an easy three-step, five-minute, daily makeup routine, and (2) watching the process more than your beauty evolution (don't close your eyes). And ask questions galore, even at the risk of being annoying. You could, for instance, query how to make your face look narrower, cheekbones more prominent, or nose smaller. Or you could find out the latest techniques of applying mascara or smudging eyeliner. The point is to stay product generic and instruction specific. If the consultant is bright, accommodating, and gracious, you might want to show your appreciation by buying a lipstick or something else you *need,* but it is certainly not obligatory.

The other instruction option is to take a makeup lesson from either a salon or store that promotes its own line of makeup, or an impartial freelance makeup artist, whose real job is to analyze your face and teach you a basic routine—not sell you products. These kinds of services can cost anywhere from $90 to $250. Aside from being rather costly, good makeup artists are hard to find. Chances are you'll have to go to one of the big city hubs to find one that's worth the investment.

Here are a few with excellent reputations. If you're not in their area, give them a call and ask for a recommendation closer to home.

*In New York:* Sandy Linter, Stephen Knoll Ltd., 625 Madison Avenue (212-421-0100); Bobbi Brown, Frederic Fekkai Beauty Center at Bergdorf Goodman, 754 Fifth Avenue (212-753-9500); and Trish McEvoy Ltd., 800 Fifth Avenue (212-758-7790).

*In Los Angeles:* Valerie Sarnelle, Valeries, 350 North Canon Drive, Beverly Hills (213-274-7348); Fiona Vallejo, Aida Thibiant, 449 North Canon Drive, Beverly Hills (213-278-7565).

*In Chicago:* Marilyn Miglin Salon, 112 East Oak Street (312-943-1120).

If money right now is too tight to even consider professional advice, your best bet is to study the how-tos in some of the beauty and fashion magazines (*Allure* is especially good in this department) and experiment on your own. Don't blow your budget on fancy cosmetics, especially during the experimental stages. When you find a product that interests you in a department store ask if trial sizes or sample packages are available—or when they will be. There are also some fine products, especially mascaras, eyeliners, and lipsticks, on your drugstore shelves that while perhaps not packaged as elegantly as the expensive name brands, are just as effective. Maybelline Great Lash mascara, for instance, always seems to get rave reviews.

Meanwhile here are a few basic tips to get you started on the right track:

*Foundations*—These should, of course, be as close as possible to your natural skin tone and applied either all over the face (very lightly) or blended in where needed. If you use a concealer, go only one or two shades lighter than your foundation. Anything lighter will give you a reverse Lone Ranger masked look. Dot on *sparingly*.

*Eyes*—Cover the lid with a light brown shadow (or tawny blush), add a line of darker shadow or pencil near the lashes, then apply mascara (hold the wand parallel to the lid close to the base of the lashes and wiggle back and forth.) *Tip:* The shadow will last longer if you apply a tiny dab of foundation or concealer to the eyelid first.

NOTE: The FDA has recently warned about using blush as eye shadow because *all* the ingredients in most blushes haven't been proven safe for use around the eye. If this sounds like a realistic concern to you, stick to regular shadow or try one of the tested double duty blush/shadows such as Estée Lauder's Just Blush Eye and Cheek Powder, or Clinique's Beyond Blusher. A lot of times I avoid shadow altogether by lining my top lid with a very soft pencil, then smudging the pencil line up into a soft shadow effect, and lightly relining.

The brows are tricky since shape is the priority. If you pluck too much or too little you could be in trouble, so go slowly. If you do need to fill in with a pencil, be sure to get one in *exactly* the right color. For more height concentrate the color on the top edge of the brow—not the bottom. For a softer, more natural brow try filling in with brown eye shadow; apply with a soft wand or minibrush.

*Lips*—Color lips, then line in natural or a *close* color for neat finished look. For longer lasting color, powder very lightly, then reapply color. (Some women prefer to line their lips first and apply color after. It's a purely personal choice.)

Red (not too bright) lips seem to be the one major exception to the general natural trend. Red can look every bit as au courant as the more natural shades, *if it works for you*. A couple of very fashion-savvy friends of mine consider red lips an indispensable accessory. They've been a signature of American Rag owner, Margo Werts' unique personal style since she was sixteen. "I feel totally uncomfortable without them," she says. "Even if I'm working in the garden and I don't put on any other makeup I still do red lips . . . always." On Margo, with her pale translucent skin, it works beautifully. Paloma Picasso too. Erin Grey, on the other hand, stays away from red. "I think red lips make me look bitchy and tight mouthed," she says. "You need full lips and a certain skin tone. I have a small mouth, not a full pouty one, so I don't want to draw attention to it. If anything, I want to draw attention to my eyes, which I think are my best feature. So I keep my lips very natural. My skin is very olive. . . . I buy lipsticks with a brown natural base."

*Again the moral: Good fashion is what works best for* you.

*Cheeks*—Choose a subtle color and follow the contour of your cheeks. Use a full soft blush brush (should be tapered to follow cheek contour). Lightly shake or blow on the brush before applying to avoid that streaked war paint clown look.

*Powder*—Most professionals set makeup with a light dusting of face powder applied with a large soft tapered brush (larger than a blush brush). *Tip:* If you simply want to reduce the shine when you're not wearing any makeup in the summer try dusting with a little baby powder.

## SKIN CARE

Skin care is just as important, if not more so, than artful makeup application, especially in these days of air pollution and ozone depletion. So your first considerations should be keeping your skin moist and protected from the elements. In the moisture department: Drink a lot of water, six to eight glasses a day should do the trick, and if you live in an extremely dry environment, sleep with a vaporizer nearby. For protection always use a moisturizer, and always apply some sort of sunblock whenever you're in the sun. The paler your skin—the higher the SPF (sun protection factor). Lying out baking in the summer sun is not only très seventies, it's just too risky in light of our environmental woes.

Monthly facials and blue-chip skin care products, needless to say, can be expensive, so if you've got an experimental nature—and a working kitchen —you might want to consider some home beauty treatments and remedies.

Here are a few simple ones that especially appeal to me:

- *Lemon juice* can help clear up pimples and minor eruptions. Apply with a cotton swab to troubled areas.
- *Potatoes* help get rid of under eye bags and puffiness. Grate raw and apply to the eye area.
- *Cider vinegar* cleans and tones the skin. Mix with equal parts of water.
- *Oatmeal* makes a good cleansing and refining mask. Mix with honey and cold cream (or milk or water) and pat on face. Let sit for fifteen minutes. Wash off with warm water.
- *Yogurt* makes a good cleansing mask for oily skin. Mix one teaspoon of yogurt with half an egg yolk, one half teaspoon of honey, and a dash of

cornstarch. Pat on face, leave for fifteen minutes. Rinse off with warm water. Use strawberry yogurt (no preservatives) for normal to dry skin.
- *Papaya and pineapple* help slough away dead skin. Crush and mix in equal parts, massage into skin, leave for twenty minutes. Rinse off with warm water.

If you're inspired by this little sampling check in your local alternative bookstore or health food store for books on the subject. A friend of mine, kitchen cosmetic queen Riquette, who you may or may not remember from her numerous appearances on the *David Letterman Show* over the years, has actually put together an oversized paperback called *Riquette's International Beauty Secrets.* It's packed full of household cosmetic recipes like the ones above. A lot of her concoctions require a few extra pinches of time and patience, but she swears (in her own inimitable style) that they're worth it. You can get her book by writing or calling: Riquette International, 211 South Robertson, Beverly Hills, CA 90211 (310-652-1333). Price: $14.95 plus $2.50 shipping.

## BODY

An aura of health and vitality is another prerequisite to a successful nineties' image, and it's one we can all afford. Eating well, exercising, and maintaining a weight that's suitable for your frame will not only make you look better in clothes, but also will make you feel better both physically and mentally.

At the risk of sounding like your mother, remember your posture. The way you stand has a monumental effect on the way your clothes drape, not to mention your overall image, so no slouching, rounded shoulders, or dropping chins allowed. The idea is look straight but relaxed. Think Fred Astaire. Simple daily stomach and stretching exercises do wonders for posture, since abdominal strength works against gravity and helps keep your body in proper alignment, and stretching keeps the muscles loose and flexible. Both show in the way you wear your clothes.

My favorite all-time yoga stretch is the Sun Salutation since almost all the muscles are brought into play. Even if you did nothing else but eight sets of these in the morning and eight at night, you'd improve your muscle tone and feeling of well-being as well.

The salutation is made up of twelve movements that flow smoothly into one another:

1. Stand straight with palms together in front of your chest, prayer position.
2. Inhale as you raise both arms over your head. Tighten buttocks as you lean back.
3. Exhale and reach out, extend downward, keeping knees straight. Touch the floor with your fingers. Bend the elbows as you lower the ribs and chest to the thighs.
4. Bend your knees, slide your right foot back. Inhale, straighten the right leg, keeping the left leg vertical.
5. Retain your breath as you slide your left foot back alongside your right. (You're now in a straight incline.)
6. Exhale, bend knees to the floor; arch back so buttocks are up in the air. Bend elbows with control from arms, and slowly lower chest and face to floor.
7. Drag yourself forward until flat on the floor. Relax the feet. Inhale as you raise your forehead, nose, chin, chest, and ribs. The lower part of the body remains on the floor from the navel down. (You're now in the Cobra position.)
8. Curl your toes under. Raise your hips until your arms and legs are straight. Exhale. Push with the palms of your hands as you lean onto your heels, flattening them against the floor. At the same time work the head toward the floor, with straight arms. (This is the Dog Down position.)
9. Shift your weight to the left hand and foot as you bring the right foot up and forward in line with your fingers. Inhale, look up, and straighten the left knee.
10. Balance on the fingers as you lift yourself up. Bring the left foot beside the right. Exhale as you place the palms of your hands down on the floor beside the feet. Straighten your legs. Bring ribs and chest down along the legs until the forehead stretches below the knees.
11. Inhale as you reach your arms out and up above your head. Stretch back.
12. Exhale as you return to original standing position.

When you repeat the salutation stress the left foot, that is, slide the left foot forward in step 4, and 9, etc. Continue to alternate each set.

For your stomach muscles try the following exercises suggested by fitness meister/Terminator Arnold Schwarzenegger in his book *Arnold's BodyShap-*

*ing for Women*. According to Arnold, this combination of bent-knee sit-ups and leg raises will tone the entire stomach—both lower and upper abdominals. He ought to know.

Place your feet under a heavy piece of furniture, such as a bed, with your legs bent at a forty-five-degree angle (to prevent the back from doing any work). Starting with your back on the floor, pull yourself up, and then let yourself back down. You should do these movements as fast as you can, establishing a smooth definite rhythm. If this exercise irritates your tailbone, sit on a folded towel.

Without resting, while still on your back, place your hands, palms down, under your buttocks and extend your legs out straight. Tuck your chin slightly and pull your legs as far as you can into your chest area. Thrust the legs back into the straight position and immediately bring them into the chest.

*Breathing:* Exhale as you sit up; inhale as you return to the floor. Exhale as you lift your legs, inhale as you lower them.

*Reps:* twenty for each exercise, increasing to fifty.

*Sets:* two for each exercise, increasing to three.

My sister Debbie the dancer agrees that stretching and stomach exercises are totally beneficial, but says the real trick to good posture is proper body alignment. She likes to think of the spine as the center of the body with three spools balanced on it: the head balanced on top of the ribs, balanced on top of the hips. It's sort of like finding your own plumb line. The actual "work" apparently comes in lifting up from the abdominals, separating your ribs from your hips, and feeling your center, or *dan tien* as t'ai chi pros call it. Alignment is a whole science unto itself and is more than we can get into here, but both good yoga and/or beginner modern dance classes are good places to find out more about it.

Meanwhile Deb recommends the "constructive rest position" for getting more in tune with your body's alignment. This one's easier than Arnold's. You just lie on your back on the floor, crook your knees up so that your feet are flat on the floor and your knees are up toward the ceiling, close your eyes, imagine your spine in the center of your body, and let the back of your neck and lower lumbar area release into the floor. While you're in the position try a few pelvic tilts. Simply lift your hips slowly into the air feeling each vertebra lifting as you go up, and settling as you go down. Don't try to arch, just let everything hang. This is also a good position for just relaxing and letting go of stress.

## GROOMING

Grooming in the nineties is more than being perfectly pressed, coiffed, and scrubbed. We all know by now that cleanliness is next to godliness. We've got that. What we haven't got is a lot of time. We're all so busy these days that it's easy to overlook those little details of personal and sartorial maintenance that keep us looking up to snuff.

So as a reminder:

- Keep your hands in good shape, nails clean and well manicured. If you wear polish, avoid over-the-top colors like indigo, and repair chips as fast as possible. And please don't bite your nails or let them grow so long that they get in your way when you button your blouse.
- Excess facial hair is not attractive on women. Either bleach it, wax it, get electrolysis, or otherwise have it looked after.
- Keep shoes clean, well polished, and well heeled. Think about having little plastic heel protectors on expensive shoes that you wear a lot.
- Shoes will last longer and look better when stored on shoe trees.
- If you're a daily panty hose wearer, always keep a fresh pair on hand (even if they're a supermarket brand). Baggy knees and/or runs are image destroyers.
- Watch hemlines. Snip any loose threads. If there's a snag, mend it before the whole hem comes undone. Make sure linings don't hang below hems. Coat and jacket linings tend to slip after a lot of wear. Check frequently and rehem if necessary.
- Watch excess perfume. A spritz is lovely, a splash divine. Saturation is déclassé.
- Hang most of your clothes on soft or contour hangers. Wire hangers often leave lines and ruin the drape of a garment. Sweaters generally should be folded, since they stretch when hung on hangers.
- Keep jewelry and metal detailing on bags and belts tarnish free and ready to be worn.
- Remind your cleaner to *hang*, not *fold*, any shirts and to hold off on the starch. Fold lines in an overstarched blouse won't help your look.
- Keep a mitt or lint brush handy to whisk away unsightly white dust particles from your dark wools.

# CHAPTER 10

# *The Coup de Grace*

## YOUR PERSONAL STYLE

Y ou're almost there. All you have to do now is add *you*—your unique spirit. True personal style goes way beyond fashion to incorporate such ineffable intangibles as wit, energy, humor, grace of movement, mannerisms, cadence of speech, values, intelligence, heart, and inner sparkle. Your clothes reflect your taste, and even, to a degree, what you're about, but they don't change your essence or substance. *Great individual style is the perfect blending of a person's essence with the clothes she chooses.* And it is as unique as a fingerprint. That's why it never works to copy another person's style lock, stock, and barrel—even if you're the same physical type. You are not her. You can, though, *learn* from those whose style you admire by analyzing and understanding *why* their fashions work for them, and then translating the principles into terms that reflect who you are.

The important thing with style is not to force it. Like Rome, great individual style isn't built in a day. It develops and matures naturally as you become more aware and astute about yourself, others, and fashion in general. With the information in this book you already have one foot up; the rest will come.

Meanwhile, keep these basics in mind:

- Wear your clothes; don't let them wear you. You want to be remembered for who you are, not for your red leather miniskirt.

*169*

- Keep it simple. If you do decide to go all out and call attention to yourself, make sure you can handle the reactions. If you wear a transparent blouse you are going to get stares and comments, plain and simple. So take responsibility for your choices. No whining allowed.
- Subtly play up your strengths. Your best qualities can be any part of the total you: skin, hair, intelligence, the timbre of your voice. Figure out what it is you like best about yourself and let it shine like a beacon. How can you play up a wonderful voice? By training it, fine-tuning it, and playing down your fashions—keeping them chic and uncomplicated. A flawless complexion? Use line and color to bring the attention to your face. (See Chapters 2 and 3.)
- Don't take the chameleon approach and try to alter your style and personality to suit the occasion—or the man in your life. Be who you are. As obvious as this sounds, becoming who you think "they" want you to be is a trap a lot of women fall into—probably because we've been programmed to try to be liked and accepted since childhood. If you're one of the millions that get ensnared in that trap it's time to escape.
- Stick with the colors, lines, and shapes that work for you. We've talked about that a lot because it's such a crucial point of individual style. If you get compliments galore every time you wear a certain shade of blue, why go looking for brown? Stick with the winners. Same goes for a neckline or a cut of slacks. By all means experiment, but don't switch until you find another comparable substitute.
- When you try new colors or shapes don't worry about making mistakes. Everybody does, even the pros. Mistakes are an inevitable part of experimentation and growth. Just take it slowly. Try new colors, lines, and styles one at a time, and mistakes and costs will be minimal. But, remember, when money is a serious issue, it's always wiser to err on the side of the practical.
- Self-awareness is a prerequisite to true style. It's important that you see and know your body and personality traits for what they are. Only then will you be able to put the fashion principles we've talked about to good use and begin to trust your fashion instincts.

I still love what late designer Willi Smith had to say about personal style when we chatted years ago. "Style is the person," he told me. "A person who believes in herself so much and is so aware of the way she wants to look that she just puts it over. People who have a great personal conviction about themselves and the way they want to look, look great. . . . Style comes from within and is simply displayed on the exterior."

Hopefully this book will help you a lot with your "exterior." But before I close, I'd like to say a quick word about our interiors too. One of the biggest battles many of us have to face is self-criticism. This decade, with its burgeoning spirit of enlightenment, is a great time to let that go and truly learn to love and appreciate ourselves. We don't have to have the most perfect proportions or the most gorgeous bone structure or be the smartest kid on the block to be a wonderful, beautiful human being. We just need to open our hearts, accept ourselves, and let our inner beauty radiate to all those around us. That's what is meant by "beauty comes from within." Of course, we all want to put our best foot forward and look as good as we can on the outside, but it's what we have on the inside that is our pièce de résistance.

# ABOUT THE AUTHOR

Leah Feldon is the author of *Dressing Rich, Womanstyle,* and *Traveling Light,* and is currently a special correspondent for *People* magazine. She has been a fashion contributor to the *Today* show, *PM Magazine, Good Morning New York, The Sonya Show, The Gary Collins Show,* and others. She also has been a fashion consultant for many companies such as Revlon, Clairol, Wrangler, Avon, Perle Vision, and Vanity Fair, and has worked with celebrities including Brooke Shields, Lauren Hutton, Cybill Shepherd, and Jerry Hall. She lives in Ojai, California.